THE NATURALLY HEALTHY GOURMET
Secrets of Quick, Tasty, and Wholesome Cooking

By Margaret Lawson
with Tom Monte

edited by Laurel Ruggles

George Ohsawa Macrobiotic Foundation
Oroville, California

Disclaimer
These recipes are offered to give you ideas and food choices for better
health. Each of us has different health needs. If you are suffering from
illness, it is suggested that you seek the advice of a physician and macrobiotic counselor.

Cover design: Carl Campbell
In-house editor: Laurel Ruggles
Book design and typesetter: Carl Ferré
Printer: Thomson-Shore, Dexter, MI

First edition 1994

Published by the George Ohsawa Macrobiotic Foundation
1511 Robinson Street, Oroville, California, 95965

Library of Congress Catalog Card Number: 94-76116
ISBN 0-918860-53-9

Printed in the United States of America

For my daughter, Janet Michelle, especially for her delightful sense of humor and loving support; my mother, Florene Wilkes; my father, S.E. Wilkes; and my sister, Dorothy Jeanene Canup, with love and gratitude.

In addition, I want to express my deep gratitude to my teachers, Michio and Aveline Kushi, Herman and Cornellia Aihara; and to Laurel Ruggles for her expertise and patience in editing this book. To my friends, especially Anne Jackson, who designed the layout of my cooking school; Romona Putman, who kitchen-tested several recipes and supported and encouraged me to complete this book; Vickye Harvey, a true and supportive friend; and to all my students and supporters along the way.

Contents

Getting Started

I believe in simplicity. It allows you to focus on the three things in cooking that really matter: making your food taste great, preparing it in the least amount of time, and choosing the ingredients that will make you and your loved ones healthier and happier.

Most people believe that healthful meals have two strikes against them: They take hours to prepare and don't taste good when you're through. The only reason many people are even willing to consider a healthy diet is because they're afraid of getting sick from the food they're already eating, or of dying from an illness they already have. But if healthy food takes forever to cook and doesn't taste good when you're finished, it's not really an answer. It's just some pie-in-the-sky idea that may or may not work. We'll never know because most of us won't do it. I wouldn't.

For five years I owned a natural-foods restaurant in Dallas, Texas. Every day, we served delicious macrobiotic food to a lot of hardworking Texans. Our clientele was as varied as wildflowers along the Rio Grande: artists, lawyers, doctors, telephone linemen, computer experts, accountants, retired ranchers, a couple of former football and basketball coaches, secretaries, bankers, and farmers. No matter what their professions, Texans are practical and down-to-earth people. If healthful food doesn't taste good, they would just as soon eat marbled beef and die whenever the good Lord calls 'em. They won't stand for a lot of talk about health if their beans and corn bread are bland.

Today at my natural-foods cooking school in Dallas, I give cooking classes to a lot of these folks and I apply the same ideas: good, hearty food that's delicious and quick-cooking. I use simple recipes, with simple ingredients and I know the secrets

7

of good home-cooked meals. And do you know what? They're the same secrets that make a successful restaurant: You can't spend hours preparing a meal; food must be simple, delicious, and healthful; and, people have to feel good when they've eaten a meal or they won't come back.

I'm going to share these secrets with you. I'm going to show you how to cook for your palate, your health, and your life — and do it simply and quickly every day. Just page through this book and you'll see that all the recipes have healthful ingredients and easy-to-follow instructions. I use these recipes every day. I have tested each of them on hundreds of people — all types of people, with all kinds of backgrounds. These are their favorites and mine, too.

When you're cooking for a lot of people every day, you learn what works and what doesn't. I recommend that you follow each recipe exactly, until you are so adept at making the dish perfectly that you can vary it according to your own desire. I'll also be warning you now and then about what can go wrong with a particular recipe.

Running a restaurant makes you keenly aware that people eat with their eyes first and their tastebuds second. The food has to look as good as it tastes. But I have found that the real proof of a meal is how you feel later on. How many times have you gone to a fancy restaurant, had a big meal, and needed some kind of potion afterwards to get your stomach and intestines to work right?

Most of us don't realize that our medical bills should be included in the price of our food, because our food is the underlying cause of most of the illnesses we suffer from. Heart disease, cancer, diabetes, high blood pressure — these and many other diseases, scientists tell us, may be caused directly by the foods we eat. See Meals That Heal, pages 199-210 for more detailed information.

Eating healthful food will save you money, time, and energy. But more importantly, it can make you clearer of mind, healthier of body, more physically beautiful, and give you a better chance at living longer. That's what macrobiotic cooking can do for you and what it has done for me.

In 1975, I began a raw-foods diet for my health. I had always been interested in food and considered myself a competent gourmet cook. But the heavy meat, fat, and sugar typical of gourmet cooking were beginning to make me ill. I had always had a mild interest in health, but I really didn't know how to change my cooking to make myself stronger. I had read that raw foods contain more enzymes and vitamins than cooked foods, and that these nutrients could make me feel better. So I decided to adopt a raw-foods diet. For six months on that diet, I felt lighter and more energetic than I had on my high-fat diet. But after those first six months I began to feel weak and chronically fatigued. I awoke each morning feeling tired, and it was downhill from there. My doctor told me that I was anemic; a daily iron supplement was all I needed, he said. I took those supplements religiously but the fatigue only got worse. All I could do was sleep. I felt useless and worthless. I went to other doctors but nothing they prescribed did one bit of good. I had zero-energy. I couldn't get through the day. After eighteen months and too many doctors, I began to believe that I would spend the rest of my life as an invalid.

One morning in the summer of 1977, I went to the health-food store to buy some carrot juice and iron pills. The store had a book sale and I noticed an odd little book with a black cover. The title of the book was *Zen Macrobiotics*, by George Ohsawa. I wasn't sure why the book attracted me so — it was an odd shape, small and thin — and the title seemed esoteric. But I bought it anyway. That book changed my life.

George Ohsawa said that daily food is the basis of health. Whole grains are the most balanced food in existence, Ohsawa said, because of how they grow and because they contain all five of the nutrient groups; vitamins, minerals, protein, fat, and carbohydrates, as well as fiber. Whole foods address the whole body. Ohsawa said that whole foods have an integrating effect on the body and mind, whereas partial food causes imbalances.

Ohsawa explained that all food can be categorized according to its effects on the body, mind, and spirit. Some foods cause organs, tissues, and cells to expand and slow down. Other foods cause the body to contract and speed up, Ohsawa said.

Ohsawa used terms from ancient Chinese philosophy; yin to describe the expanding force and yang to describe the contracting force. He characterized foods according to these two complementary forces. An example of a food having expanding or yin qualities is sugar, which can make the mind go out of focus and the nervous system slow down. Consequently, all physical and mental activity is affected by sugar consumption. On the other hand, salt can cause blood vessels to narrow, cells to contract, and blood pressure to be elevated. Salt has contracting, or yang qualities.

Ohsawa maintained that all food could be placed on a spectrum of yin and yang. Among the most expansive foods are drugs. (Many are said to be "mind-expanding.") One of the most yang or contractive foods on earth is salt. Ohsawa said that health is established by eating foods such as whole grains and fresh vegetables that are located at or reasonably near the midpoint between extreme yin and extreme yang.

Food's contractive or expansive effect causes each of us to have a generally more expanded or more contracted physical condition. People who eat lots of sweets, drink alcohol, or smoke marijuana tend to have more expanded, relaxed, or passive conditions. They also may suffer from a variety of illnesses associated with the use of these substances, such as hypoglycemia, weakened immune systems, chronic colds, and viral infections. On the other hand, people who eat more salt, meat, and other animal products generally have more contracted conditions, and thus are more active, determined, and aggressive. They may suffer from illnesses related to their dietary choices, such as heart disease, high blood pressure, and colon and/or prostate cancer.

Ohsawa maintained that cooking makes food more yang, while raw foods are more yin. Therefore, a raw-foods diet such as the one I was following could make me progressively weaker, anemic, and out of focus.

The philosophy of yin and yang made sense to me. That summer of 1977 I adopted a macrobiotic way of eating. My diet was made up of a variety of whole grains such as brown rice, barley, wheat, corn, oats, and buckwheat; fresh vegetables, especially leafy greens, roots, and squash; beans such as azuki, chickpeas, black, pinto, navy, lentils, limas, and soybeans; sea vegetables including hijiki, arame, dulse, nori, and wakame; several fermented products such as pickles, sauerkraut, natural soy sauce, and miso; and small amounts of fish, fruit, and a variety of natural sweeteners such as barley malt and rice syrup. By the end of summer, my health had markedly improved. I had increasing energy and stamina and within two years I had completely recovered.

Because of my almost miraculous recovery through a macrobiotic way of eating, I continued to study macrobiotics. I also organized seminars and began teaching macrobiotic cooking out of my home. Soon, I had fifty regular students and needed larger cooking facilities and classroom space. Once I was in larger quarters my classes continued to grow.

In 1987, the number of people who attended my classes regularly was large enough to convince me that a macrobiotic restaurant in the Dallas area would be successful. So, in September of that year, I opened a little place and it prospered. Today, while I continue teaching, I remain close to my students and I know their concerns. Like most of us today, they are concerned about their health.

It was during the early- to mid-1980s that the diet-and-health connection was beginning to take hold in the American consciousness. Many people realized that they couldn't go on eating steak, potatoes, and sugar and expect to be healthy. What they couldn't part with was good-tasting food. Also, they couldn't bear the thought of staying in the kitchen all day. The vast majority of the people who attended my classes then, as now, had jobs. They didn't have the time or the energy to spend all night in the kitchen when they got home from work. Macrobiotics had to be practical for these people, otherwise they just weren't interested. I learned to make it practical.

Here are some tips to help you get started.

The first is a must: You've got to have leftover whole grain in your refrigerator. That way, you can come home, take your grain from the refrigerator, and simply reheat it by steaming over boiling water. You can also try a stir-fried rice dish by adding a few vegetables and quickly sautéing all the ingredients in an oiled skillet.

Grain is one of the foods that require the most preparation time, so make a lot of it. A big pot of grain can last three days and two pots per week is all you really need to make. Do the same with beans. Cook big pots of beans two or three times a week and reheat for lunch or dinner. You can also use leftover beans to make chickpea dip or add leftover beans to soup. Leftover beans and grain can become burgers, a fun dish, especially for kids.

Cook with small amounts of sea salt, which provides trace minerals and acts as a wonderful preservative. It will increase the length of time your grains and beans remain tasty.

Before you refrigerate cooked grains or beans, let them sit out on your counter until they reach room temperature. If you refrigerate them before they reach room temperature—that is, while they're still hot—they'll go sour in the refrigerator.

When preparing for a trip, cook rice with an umeboshi, a pickled plum which serves as a very effective preservative, keeping the rice from spoiling even when not refrigerated.

When boiling beans, don't add sea salt until the beans are 80 percent done, otherwise they will remain hard. Put a stalk of kombu seaweed in the pot of beans and water when you turn

on the flame. Cook the beans and seaweed together; the seaweed will soften the beans and make them more digestible.
When the beans are nearly done, add salt.

Cook seaweed in large quantities and refrigerate leftovers;
seaweed will keep three to four days. Leftover seaweed can be
turned into a nice salad by adding a vinegrated dressing. Use
sushi nori to make sushi rolls or rice balls. Sushi nori is already
toasted and requires no preparation.

Use good-quality udon or whole-wheat noodles. Udon is a
sifted-whole-wheat pasta; light, delicious, and very much like
spaghetti. Noodles take about fifteen minutes to cook. You can
combine them with a variety of vegetables and broth to make a
hearty and healing meal.

When you bake, place the dry ingredients in one bowl and
the wet ingredients in another. Let's say you're making carob
brownies: Place the flour, carob, baking powder, and salt in one
bowl; the liquid sweetener, oil, and vanilla in a second bowl;
and the nuts and raisins in a third. Preheat the oven and oil the
pans before you fold the ingredients together in a mixing bowl.
Don't mix the ingredients until you're certain that everything
else is ready. (If your friend calls, say you'll call back.) The minute you mix the wet and dry ingredients, the flour begins to rise
and soften. If you don't get the batch into the heated oven
promptly, your brownies will be bricks.

Be organized. Have food and utensils in their places so you
can find them when you need them. Unnecessary objects on
your counters will just confuse you and slow you down. For additional tips, including buying the right equipment, see The
Cooking Environment, pages 211-216.

Cooking is an adventure. It's a little different every time you
do it. Be creative and don't be afraid to make mistakes. Recent-
ly, I created a creamy millet pie that turned out bland because I
didn't add enough sweetener. I offered it to one of my regulars
and asked him what he thought. "It's alright," he said. "I
wouldn't turn it down, but I wouldn't pay money for it either."

I carefully removed the millet filling from the pie shell and blenderized it with added lemon zest and a jar of organic apricot jam. When it was creamy, I transferred the contents into the same pie shell and turned the whole thing into apricot lemon pie. I served it to the same man and he wanted to buy the whole pie on the spot. Sometimes your mistakes can turn into something special.

Cooking is one of the most important jobs you can have because you are determining the health of those who eat your food regularly. Use quality ingredients, follow the recipes accurately, and you'll change people's lives. I can whip up a delicious, healthful meal in thirty minutes that will make you feel good. If you read this book and follow these recipes, you can, too.

Soups

If you want people to relax and feel welcome, put soup in front of them. Soup slows you down. It whispers to you to concentrate on your food. Don't rush through your meal. Relax. You're home.

Soup is one of my specialties. I always offer soup to my guests because I know if they eat a bowl of soup before their meal, they will eat slowly and enjoy the food. The soup will improve their digestion and they'll feel better.

There are many different soup stocks, but one of the best is miso. Miso is made from beans and grain—usually soybeans and rice or soybeans and barley—along with salt and koji. But other beans and grains can be used, such as chickpeas and millet. One or another of these combinations is naturally aged in wooden barrels under just the right conditions to create an incredibly healthful fermented paste. This paste is used as the base for soups, sauces, stews, gravies, and dressings.

The Japanese, who invented miso, say it "strengthens the weak and softens the hard." What they mean is that it restores vitality and endurance, while softening and dissolving stones, tension, and hardness in the body. Miso soup has been studied by the Japanese National Cancer Institute, which found a reduced incidence of cancer among those who eat it regularly.

Miso provides friendly bacteria, which assist and strengthen digestion and make nutrients more accessible to the small intestine and bloodstream. Miso is one of the most strength-giving foods you can eat and I recommend it highly.

Here are some soups to help you relax, slow down time, and welcome a loved one home.

Great Northern Bean Soup

This soup is special. The addition of thyme gives it a savory taste. For an even richer flavor, the onions may be sautéed in two teaspoons sesame oil.

> **2 cups great northern beans**
> **4 to 5 cups water, for soaking**
> **6 cups water, for cooking**
> **1 strip kombu, 4 inches long and 1 inch wide**
> **1 bay leaf**
> **3 onions (minced)**
> **2 carrots (diced)**
> **2 ribs celery (thinly sliced)**
> **1½ to 2 tsp. sea salt**
> **½ tsp. dried thyme**
> **¼ tsp. poultry seasoning**

1. Wash beans and soak overnight in 4 to 5 cups water.
2. Drain and wash again, discarding soaking water.
3. Place beans, kombu, and bay leaf in large soup pot with 6 cups fresh water. Bring to a boil.
4. Add onions. Lower flame. Cover and simmer about 1 hour or until beans are soft.
5. Add remaining ingredients. Cover and simmer 15 to 20 minutes longer.

Servings: 7 or 8

Red Bean Soup

Red beans and rice is a traditional southern dish, so I sometimes place a scoop of brown rice in the center of a large bowl of Red Bean Soup. Served with a square of corn bread and a slice of red onion, it is sure to please everyone. Vegetables may be sautéed in 2 tablespoons oil before adding for a more flavorful soup.

$1\frac{1}{2}$ cups red beans
4 to 5 cups water, for soaking
6 cups water, for cooking
1 strip kombu, 4 inches long and 1 inch wide
2 onions (coarsely chopped)
2 carrots (finely diced)
2 ribs celery (thinly sliced)
$\frac{1}{4}$ bunch parsley (chopped)
2 cloves garlic (minced)
1 Tbsp. cumin
$\frac{1}{2}$ tsp. oregano
1 bay leaf
1 to $1\frac{1}{2}$ tsp. sea salt

1. Wash beans and soak overnight in 4 to 5 cups water.
2. Drain beans and wash again, discarding soaking water.
3. Cover beans with 6 cups fresh water and add kombu. Bring to a boil.
4. Add onions. Lower flame. Cover and simmer $1\frac{1}{2}$ hours or until beans are tender.
5. Add remaining ingredients. Cover and simmer until vegetables are tender.

Servings: 4 or 5

Green Split Pea and Barley Soup

I've made this soup once a week for the past four years without changing it, since I can't improve on a good thing.

2 cups green split peas (washed and drained)
8 to 9 cups water
1 bay leaf
2 Tbsp. barley
2 onions (chopped)
2 tsp. oil
1 clove garlic (minced)
2 carrots (grated)
1 tsp. dried thyme
1½ tsp. sea salt
2 tsp. brown-rice miso
½ bunch parsley (chopped)

1. Bring peas to a boil in 8 to 9 cups water with bay leaf and barley.
2. Lower flame. Cover and simmer 25 minutes.
3. Meanwhile, sauté onions in oil about 5 minutes.
4. Add onions, garlic, and carrots. Cover and simmer 25 minutes or until peas are tender.
5. Add thyme and salt.
6. Purée miso in a small amount of water and add to pot.
7. Simmer 10 minutes longer, stirring to keep peas from sticking.
8. Add parsley just before serving.

Servings: 7 or 8

Yellow Split Pea and Barley Soup

Since split peas require no soaking, this is one of the easiest soups to prepare. It will cook in about one hour.

2 cups yellow split peas (washed and drained)
8 to 9 cups water
1 bay leaf
2 Tbsp. barley
3 onions (chopped)
2 tsp. oil
3 cloves garlic (minced)
1 carrot (grated)
1 tsp. dried marjoram
1/2 tsp. dried rosemary
1 1/2 tsp. sea salt
2 tsp. brown-rice miso

1. Bring peas to a boil in 8 to 9 cups water with bay leaf and barley.
2. Lower flame. Cover and simmer 25 minutes. (Add 1/2 cup additional water if thinner soup is desired.)
3. While peas are simmering, sauté onions in oil about 5 minutes.
4. Add onions, garlic, and carrot to soup. Cover and simmer 25 minutes or until peas are tender.
5. Add marjoram, rosemary, and salt.
6. Purée miso in a small amount of water and add to pot.
7. Simmer 10 minutes longer, stirring to keep peas from sticking.

Servings: 7 or 8

Red Lentil Soup

This soup is a favorite. Try leftover Red Lentil Soup as a sauce over grain or patties.

2 cups red lentils (washed and drained)
8 to 9 cups water
2 onions (finely cut)
2 tsp. oil
2 carrots (grated)
2 to 2½ tsp. sea salt
1 Tbsp. brown-rice miso, puréed in ¼ cup water
3 Tbsp. canola oil
1 tsp. black mustard seeds
1 tsp. cumin seeds
1 tsp. turmeric
2 Tbsp. ginger juice (squeezed from grated fresh ginger root)

1. Bring lentils to a boil in 8 to 9 cups water.
2. Sauté onions in 2 teaspoons oil.
3. Add onions and grated carrots to soup. Cover and simmer 30 minutes.
4. Season with salt and miso.
5. Heat canola oil in a small saucepan until hot. Add mustard seeds, cumin seeds, and turmeric, stirring constantly. Watch carefully to avoid burning spices. Remove saucepan from flame after 30 seconds. Transfer roasted spices to soup pot.
6. Add ginger juice. Stir very well to combine the flavors.
7. Taste and adjust salt if needed.

Servings: 7 or 8

Basic Miso Soup

1 onion (cut in lengthwise crescents)

1 thin slice fresh ginger root
3 cups water
2 strips wakame, 4 inches long and 1 inch wide (soaked
     and sliced)
1 carrot (thinly sliced)
1 Tbsp. barley miso
2 scallions (thinly sliced)

1. Place 1 inch water in a soup pot. Add onion and ginger. Cover and simmer 15 minutes, or until onion is tender.
2. Add remaining water, wakame, and carrot. Cover and simmer 7 or 8 minutes.
3. Purée miso in $1/4$ cup broth from soup pot.
4. Stir the puréed miso into the soup. Simmer 3 minutes.
5. Serve garnished with scallions.
Yield: 3 cups

Daikon Wakame Miso Soup

4 to 5 cups water
3 strips wakame, 4 inches long and 1 inch wide (soaked
     and sliced)
1 cup daikon (cut in thin half-moons)
4 tsp. barley miso
2 Tbsp. scallions (chopped)

1. Place the water in a saucepan and bring to a boil.
2. Add the wakame. Reduce the flame to medium low. Cover and simmer about 3 minutes.
3. Add the daikon. Cover and simmer 2 to 3 minutes longer or until the daikon is tender. Reduce the flame to low.
4. Purée miso in $1/4$ cup of the soup stock. Stir the puréed miso into the soup. Cover and simmer 2 to 3 minutes.
5. Garnish each bowl of soup with 1 teaspoon scallions.
Servings: 5 or 6

Butternut Squash Miso Soup

1 onion (thinly sliced)
4 to 5 cups water
2 cups butternut squash (peeled and cubed)
2 Tbsp. mellow white miso

1. Place onion and 1 cup water in a pot. Cover and simmer 20 minutes.
2. Add squash and remaining water.
3. Bring back to a boil. Reduce flame. Cover and simmer until squash is tender, about 15 minutes.
4. Purée miso in $\frac{1}{4}$ cup of soup stock and add to soup. Simmer 2 minutes before serving.

Servings: 3 or 4

Creamy Butternut Squash Soup

2 onions (chopped)
8 cups butternut squash (peeled and cubed)
water to cover
2 Tbsp. mellow white miso
2 tsp. ginger juice (squeezed from grated fresh ginger root)

1. Layer onions, then squash in a soup pot.
2. Add enough water to just cover the vegetables. Bring to a boil.
3. Reduce flame. Cover and simmer gently 45 minutes.
4. Purée miso in $\frac{1}{4}$ cup of the soup broth and add to soup. Stir in the ginger juice.
5. Taste and adjust seasoning, adding more miso if necessary.
6. Simmer 2 to 3 minutes before serving.

Servings: 6

Carrot and Oat Soup

6 cups water
6 carrots (sliced)
1 cup oat flakes
1 Tbsp. mellow-white miso
1 cup boiling water

1. Bring 6 cups water to a boil and add carrots. Reduce heat.
2. Cover and simmer 20 minutes or until carrots are tender.
3. Add oat flakes and stir to combine. Cover and simmer 15 minutes.
4. Purée miso in 1 cup boiling water and stir into soup.
5. Taste and adjust seasoning if necessary.

Servings: 5 or 6

Watercress Soup

4 to 5 cups water
1 strip kombu, 6 to 8 inches long and 1 inch wide
2 to 3 Tbsp. natural soy sauce
1 bunch watercress (washed)

1. Place the water and kombu in a pot and allow kombu to soak for 3 to 5 minutes.
2. Bring to a boil. Cover and reduce the flame to medium low. Simmer about 10 minutes
3. Remove the kombu. Set the kombu aside to use in a future dish.
4. Reduce the flame to low. Add the soy sauce.
5. Place 2 or 3 sprigs of watercress in each individual soup bowl.
6. Pour 1 to 1½ ladles of hot broth over the raw watercress. The heat from the broth will cook the watercress in seconds.

Servings: 4

Noodles and Broth

2 shiitake mushrooms
4¼ cups water
1 strip kombu, 5 inches long and 1 inch wide
3 to 4 Tbsp. natural soy sauce
7 to 8 oz. udon noodles (cooked)
2 scallions (thinly sliced)

1. Soak shiitake in water 30 minutes, in a saucepan.
2. Add kombu. Cover and simmer 10 minutes.
3. Remove kombu and shiitake and save for another soup stock.
4. Add soy sauce to broth. Cover and simmer 3 minutes.
5. Place cooked noodles in individual serving bowls and pour hot broth over them.
7. Garnish with scallions.

Servings: 3

Grains

When I was a little girl, I used to spend parts of my summers at my grandfather's vegetable farm in Alabama. He'd start working his fields before the sun came up each morning and in the afternoons he'd rest in his hammock out back. My grandmother seemed forever in her huge country kitchen. I can't recall her smiling face without seeing her in her apron, shelling peas, shucking corn, or baking whole-grain bread. Each afternoon, she'd prepare some of the vast bounty that came right off the farm. In the summer, we ate sweet corn. My grandmother would put a big pot of water on the stove, get it boiling, and then tell someone — often it was me — to run out and pick some fresh corn, right off the stalks. We'd shuck it and put it in the boiling water and watch it turn golden. That was the sweetest corn I have ever eaten, in more ways than one.

On Sundays, my grandparents would host a table full of friends and relatives. It was like a weekly Thanksgiving feast. The colors on that table were as rich and diverse as the palate of a great artist. Both my grandparents lived well into their nineties. To this day, I associate my grandparents with wise eating and whole grains.

Whole grains, of course, contain all the nutrients — the vitamins, minerals, protein, carbohydrate, fat, and fiber — that nature placed in them. Whole grains have not been refined, which is to say, stripped of their inherent goodness during processing. Consequently, they still possess the germ, the nutrient-rich part of the grain. First and foremost, whole grains are energy foods. They are rich sources of complex carbohydrates, now recognized by many as the best source of energy available to the human body. Complex carbohydrates provide long-lasting energy, the kind that endures through the day. Refined white sugars and white flours burn quickly and leave us feeling exhausted, irritable, and moody in a short time. Studies have shown that whole grain increases brain levels of serotonin, a chemical neu-rotransmitter that gives people a feeling of calm and well-being. It also helps focus the mind and provide better sleep.

Whole grains also provide fiber, which helps speed diges-tion, eliminate waste, and maintain the health of the intestinal tract. The fiber in many grains, especially in rice and oats, is called soluble fiber, which binds with cholesterol and fats to lower blood cholesterol. Diets deficient in fiber are associated with greater incidences of breast and colon cancers. (See Meals That Heal, pages 199-205.) Grains provide protein, B vitamins, and minerals, such as iron.

Grain is comforting and strengthening. It gives me the feel-ing that I can take on the day and meet whatever comes my way. It anchors the other foods. It provides bulk and weight so that I feel satisfied but never stuffed. It never makes me feel weighed down or exhausted after a meal. For me, no meal is complete without grain. It's the hub of every meal.

Tips for Preparing Grain

Grain is versatile and easily stored. You can place brown rice, wheat, barley, or oats in jars and leave them there for months, even years, without worrying about them spoiling. (You can get weevils and other insects, however, so keep your grains in a cool, dry place and use them often.) Always cook grains with a pinch of sea salt. Salt opens up the grain and gives it a nuttier flavor.

One of the myths of natural-foods cooking is that grain takes forever to prepare. Actually, there are faster- and slower-cooking grains. Quinoa, amaranth, and bulgur can be prepared in fifteen minutes. Couscous is the grain that's prepared the fastest of all: boil water, add the couscous, and steam for five minutes. Pasta is a delicious and quick-cooking grain.

One of my favorite meals is noodles and broth. Here's how I make it: While the noodles are boiling, I take another saucepan and boil some slivered carrot, sliced ginger root and scallions, one shiitake mushroom, and a strip of kombu seaweed. Simmer for ten to fifteen minutes and then add soy sauce. Put the noodles in a serving bowl and pour this wonderful broth over the top. A wholesome and delicious meal in a single bowl—and in less than twenty minutes.

Leftover grain can be reheated in a steamer in five to ten minutes. Therefore, I always cook more grain than I actually need for any particular meal.

What all of this boils down to is this: preparing delicious, wholesome, and nutritious whole grain doesn't mean that you're tied to the kitchen for hours. You can have a delicious grain feast as fast as you can a standard American meal. All you need is a little knowledge and preparation. As for variety, leftover grains can be turned into croquettes, loaves, and patties, or stuffed into burritos. Their flavors can be enhanced or multipled by a rainbow of sauces and gravies, which I have provided in Sauces and Dressings, pages 144-170. Most of these sauces can be prepared in minutes. So there are no excuses! Grain is easy, delicious, and fun.

Boiled Brown Rice

> **2 cups water**
> **1 cup short-grain brown rice (washed and drained)**
> **¼ tsp. sea salt**

1. Bring water to a boil.
2. Add brown rice and salt.
3. Bring to a second boil and lower flame. Cover and place a heat diffuser under the pot.
4. Simmer 45 to 50 minutes.
5. Turn flame off. Leave covered 5 minutes before serving.
Servings: 4

Pressure-Cooked Brown Rice

3 cups short-grain brown rice (washed and drained)
4½ cups water
1 pinch sea salt per cup of rice

1. Place all ingredients in a pressure cooker and fasten down the cover.
2. Turn the flame to high and bring to full pressure.
3. Reduce the flame to medium low and place a heat diffuser under the pressure cooker. Cook for 50 minutes.
4. Turn the flame off and allow the pressure to come down naturally.
5. When the pressure is completely down, remove cover and transfer the rice to a serving bowl.

Servings: 6

Pressure-Cooked Brown Rice and Barley

2½ cups short-grain brown rice (washed and drained)
½ cup barley (washed and soaked 6 to 8 hours)
4½ cups water
1 pinch sea salt per cup of grain

1. Place all ingredients in a pressure cooker and fasten down the cover.
2. Turn the flame to high and bring to full pressure.
3. Reduce the flame to medium low and place a heat diffuser under the pressure cooker. Cook for 50 minutes.
4. Turn the flame off and allow the pressure to come down naturally.
5. When the pressure is down completely, remove cover and transfer the grain to a serving bowl.

Servings: 6

Pressure-Cooked Brown Rice and Millet

2 cups brown rice (washed and drained)
1 cup millet (washed and drained)
$4\frac{1}{2}$ cups of water
1 pinch sea salt per cup of grain

1. Place all ingredients in a pressure cooker and fasten down the cover.
2. Turn the flame to high and bring to full pressure.
3. Reduce the flame to medium low and place a heat diffuser under the pressure cooker. Cook for 50 minutes.
4. Turn the flame off and allow the pressure to come down naturally.
5. When the pressure is completely down, remove the cover and transfer the grain to a serving bowl.

Servings: 6

Instant Rice "Muffin"

$2\frac{1}{4}$ cups freshly-cooked short-grain brown rice
3 Tbsp. pumpkin seeds (lightly roasted)
$\frac{3}{4}$ cup sautéed vegetables (such as carrots, yellow squash, scallions; cut small)

1. Wet a rice mold. (Any eight-ounce bowl or cup may be used as a mold.)
2. For each "muffin," layer 1 tablespoon seeds, followed by $\frac{1}{4}$ cup vegetables, then $\frac{3}{4}$ cup rice in the mold.
3. Press down firmly to make a compact "muffin."
4. Invert and unmold on a serving plate.
5. Make 2 more "muffins" in the same manner.

Servings: 3

Brown Rice and Lentils

I often prepare this dish on my day off. It's a quick one-pot meal that allows me to spend minimal time in the kitchen.

4¼ cups water
½ tsp. sea salt
1 onion (chopped)
1½ cups brown rice (washed and drained)
½ cup lentils (washed and drained)
1 carrot (cubed)
¼ cup sunflower seeds
1 bay leaf

1. Bring water to a boil in a saucepan.
2. Add remaining ingredients and bring to a second boil.
3. Lower flame. Cover and cook 45 minutes.
4. Turn flame off and leave covered 5 to 10 minutes before serving.

Servings: 4

Lima Bean and Rice Pilaf

1¼ cups water
½ tsp. sea salt
2 Tbsp. celery (chopped)
4 Tbsp. onion (minced)
4 dried apple slices (chopped)
½ cup brown rice (washed and drained)
½ cup frozen lima beans

1. Bring water to a boil. Add salt, celery, onion, and apple.
2. When water returns to a boil, add brown rice and lima beans.
3. Cover and simmer over low flame 40 to 45 minutes.

Servings: 2 or 3

Wild and Long-Grain Brown Rice

4 cups water
$\frac{1}{2}$ tsp. sea salt
$\frac{1}{2}$ cup wild rice (washed and drained)
$1\frac{1}{2}$ cups long-grain brown rice (washed and drained)

1. Bring water to a boil.
2. Add sea salt and both the wild and brown rice.
3. When water returns to boil, reduce flame. Cover and simmer 45 minutes.
4. Turn flame off and leave covered 5 minutes before serving.

Servings: 4 or 5

Rice with Scallions and Nori

1 Tbsp. toasted sesame oil
1 cup onion (minced)
3 cups cooked brown rice
2 tsp. natural soy sauce
1 sheet nori (toasted)
4 scallions (sliced)
1 tsp. ginger juice (squeezed from grated fresh ginger root)

1. Heat skillet over medium-high flame. Add oil and onions.
2. Sauté onions until limp, about 5 minutes.
3. Stir cooked rice into onions. Cover and reduce flame to low. Place heat diffuser under the skillet. Simmer until heated through, about 10 minutes.
4. Add soy sauce. Cook another 3 minutes.
5. Cut toasted nori into 1x3-inch strips.
6. Mix nori, scallions, and ginger juice into the rice.

Servings: 4 or 5

Three-Grain Pilaf

Tired of the standard grain fare? This is a nice change of pace.

> **1 onion (minced)**
> **2 garlic cloves (minced)**
> **1 Tbsp. sesame oil**
> **1¾ cups vegetable broth**
> **½ tsp. sea salt**
> **¼ cup bulgur**
> **¼ cup brown rice (washed and drained)**
> **¼ cup barley (washed and drained)**
> **¼ cup parsley (minced)**

1. Sauté onion and garlic in oil about 5 minutes.
2. Add vegetable broth and bring to a boil.
3. Add salt, bulgur, brown rice, and barley.
4. Bring to a second boil. Cover and simmer gently 45 minutes.
5. Stir in parsley. Cover and let stand 5 minutes before serving.

Servings: 3

Soft and Sweet Barley with Spelt

A great breakfast.

> **3¾ cups water**
> **¼ tsp. sea salt**
> **1 cup butternut squash (cubed)**
> **1 cup carrots (cubed)**
> **¾ cup barley (washed and drained)**
> **¼ cup spelt (washed and drained)**

1. Bring water to a boil in pressure cooker.
2. Add remaining ingredients.
3. When pot returns to boil, attach lid and bring to full pressure. Place heat diffuser under cooker. Simmer 45 minutes.
4. Allow pressure to come down. Remove lid and serve.

Servings: 4 or 5

Bulgur with Shiitake Sauce

½ cup onions (chopped)
1 Tbsp. corn oil
1 cup bulgur
2 cups water
½ tsp. sea salt

Shiitake Sauce

½ cup water
2 cups fresh shiitake mushrooms (cut in matchsticks)
1 cup cauliflower (cut in flowerets)
1 cup carrots (cut in matchsticks)
1 Tbsp. kuzu, dissolved in ½ cup water
½ tsp. dried thyme
½ tsp. dried rosemary
2 tsp. natural soy sauce

1. Sauté onions in oil until tender.
2. Add bulgur and sauté 1 or 2 minutes.
3. Add 2 cups water and salt.
4. Bring to a boil and reduce heat. Cover and simmer 15 minutes.
5. To make sauce, combine ½ cup water, shiitake, cauliflower, and carrots in a second saucepan.
6. Cover and cook 6 minutes.
7. Combine dissolved kuzu with thyme, rosemary, and soy sauce.
8. Stir the kuzu mixture into the vegetables. Simmer 1 minute, stirring constantly.
9. To serve, place a scoop of bulgur on each plate and top with shiitake sauce.

Servings: 3 or 4

Bulgur Helper

Try using this in Mexican Chalupas, tacos, spaghetti, chili, and casseroles. It will keep four or five days stored in a covered container and refrigerated.

> **4 cups water**
> **2 cups bulgur**
> **¼ tsp. sea salt**
> **2 tsp. granulated onion**
> **2 tsp. granulated garlic**
> **2 to 3 Tbsp. natural soy sauce**

1. Bring water to a boil. Add bulgur and salt.
2. Cover and bring back to boil. Lower flame and simmer 20 minutes.
3. Stir in the onion and garlic.
4. Transfer bulgur mixture to an oiled baking sheet.
5. Sprinkle generously with soy sauce (or use a spray bottle).
6. Bake uncovered in a 300-degree oven for 30 minutes.
7. Let cool.

Yield: 8 cups

Bulgur Shiitake Pilaf

Quick and delicious.

> **1 onion (sliced in lengthwise crescents)**
> **2 Tbsp. toasted sesame oil**
> **4 shiitake mushrooms (soaked and sliced)**
> **2 cups water**
> **2 Tbsp. natural soy sauce**
> **1 cup bulgur**
> **½ bunch parsley (chopped)**
> **½ cup peanuts (roasted)**

1. Sauté onions in oil until soft.

2. Add shiitake and sauté a few minutes together with the onions.
3. Add water and soy sauce. Bring to a boil and reduce flame.
   Cover and simmer 3 minutes.
4. Add bulgur and bring back to a boil. Lower flame. Cover and
   simmer gently 15 minutes.
5. Turn off flame and leave covered for 10 minutes.
6. Stir in parsley and peanuts.

Servings: 3

Peanut Butter Corn Grits

Children really go for this one.

>**1 onion (minced)**
>**1 carrot (finely chopped)**
>**1 pinch sea salt**
>**2 cups Old-Fashioned Cornmeal Porridge, page 37**
>**$1/4$ cup peanut butter**
>**$1/3$ cup unbleached flour**
>**2 Tbsp. sesame oil**

1. Water-sauté onion and carrot with a pinch of salt until tender.
2. Drain the vegetables and add them to Porridge.
3. Stir in the peanut butter and mix well.
4. Transfer the mixture to a loaf pan and chill until firm.
5. Turn the chilled loaf out on a cutting board and slice.
6. Sprinkle each slice with flour and fry in oil until brown on
   both sides.

Servings: 6 to 8

Texas-Style Polenta

A standard part of my cooking classes, this dish was created using a heavy cast-iron pot with enamel interior. This heavy pot retains heat and will continue cooking the food for several minutes after the flame has been turned off. If you are cooking this polenta in a regular stainless-steel pot, it should be simmered another five minutes before turning the flame off.

> **2 onions (chopped)**
> **1 Tbsp. corn oil**
> **4 cups water**
> **$\frac{1}{2}$ tsp. sea salt**
> **2 carrots (grated)**
> **kernels cut from 2 ears corn**
> **1 cup yellow corn grits**

1. Sauté onions in oil until transparent. Add a few grains of salt to the onions while sautéing to help soften them.
2. When onion is soft, add water and remaining salt.
3. Bring water to a boil. Add carrots and corn.
4. When pot returns to a boil, whisk in the corn grits, stirring constantly to avoid lumping. Continue to stir until the mixture thickens.
5. Cover and simmer over low flame 15 minutes.
6. Turn flame off and leave lid on pot for 5 minutes to allow steam to finish the cooking process.

Servings: 3

Old-Fashioned Cornmeal Porridge

$^3/_4$ cup yellow cornmeal
$^1/_2$ tsp. sea salt
$2^3/_4$ cups boiling water

1. Add cornmeal and salt to boiling water and cook 5 minutes, stirring constantly.
2. Lower flame and place a heat diffuser under pot. Cover and simmer 50 minutes, stirring occasionally to prevent sticking.
3. Turn flame off and leave covered 5 minutes before serving.

Servings: 2

Dilled Couscous with Limas

This is a one-pot meal, best cooked in a two-quart cast-iron pot with enamel interior.

2 onions (chopped)
1 Tbsp. sesame oil
$1^1/_2$ cups water
$^1/_4$ tsp. sea salt
10 oz. frozen baby lima beans (thawed)
1 tsp. dried dill weed
1 cup couscous

1. Sauté onions in oil until very soft. Add a few grains of salt to the onions while sautéing.
2. When onions are soft, add water and remaining salt. Bring to a boil.
3. Add lima beans and dill weed. Cover and simmer 5 minutes.
4. Add couscous and simmer 1 minute.
5. Turn flame off and leave covered for 5 minutes.
6. Remove cover and stir to fluff up before serving.

Servings: 3

Cracked-Wheat Porridge

When friends ask my advice on what to eat for sluggish intestines, this dish is my answer. This porridge is a fermented food providing friendly bacteria to help get things moving. Have the porridge for breakfast for five consecutive days and make it fresh each day. Nothing else should be eaten until lunch time. I admit it sounds like a strange breakfast but it actually tastes very good. (Garlic may be omitted if desired.)

> 6 Tbsp. cracked wheat
> water to cover
> 1 Tbsp. natural sauerkraut
> 1 clove garlic (minced)
> 1 Tbsp. tahini
> ¼ tsp. natural soy sauce

1. Place cracked wheat in a saucepan. Add water to cover and place a bamboo mat over the pan.
2. Allow to soak 24 hours. After soaking, the cracked wheat should smell slightly sour and may have absorbed all the water. If so, add just enough fresh water to cover.
3. Add sauerkraut and garlic. Simmer over low flame for 5 minutes.
4. Add tahini and soy sauce. Simmer 1 to 2 minutes, stirring constantly.

Servings: 1

My Favorite Millet Medley

> 1 onion (chopped)
> 2 tsp. sesame oil
> 1 carrot (cut in small cubes)
> ½ butternut squash (cut in small cubes)
> ½ head cauliflower (coarsely chopped)

4 cups water
1/2 tsp. sea salt
1 cup millet (washed and drained)

1. Sauté onion in oil using a heavy Dutch oven or other heavy pot.
2. Add remaining ingredients except millet. Bring to a boil.
3. Stir in millet. Lower flame and place a heat diffuser under the pot. Simmer gently for 45 minutes.

Servings: 4 or 5

One-Pot Millet Stew

Try serving this stew with corn bread and split pea soup.

8 cups water
2 Tbsp. natural soy sauce
2 cups millet (washed and drained)
1 cup cauliflower (coarsely chopped)
2 cloves garlic (minced)
2 ribs celery (sliced)
1 carrot (cut in rounds)
1 onion (chopped)
1/4 tsp. dried rosemary
1/4 tsp. dried sage
1/4 tsp. dried basil
1/2 tsp. sea salt

1. Bring water and soy sauce to a boil.
2. Add remaining ingredients. Lower flame and place heat diffuser under pot. Cover and simmer 45 minutes.
3. Turn flame off and leave covered 5 minutes.

Servings: 6

Hearty Millet Porridge

> 2¾ cups water
> ½ onion (chopped)
> 1 cup butternut squash (cubed)
> ¼ tsp. sea salt
> ½ cup millet (washed and drained)
> ¼ cup lentils (washed and drained)

1. Place water in pot and bring to a boil.
2. Add remaining ingredients.
3. Bring back to boil. Lower flame and place heat diffuser under pot.
4. Cover and simmer 40 minutes.
5. Turn flame off and leave covered 10 minutes.
6. Stir to combine ingredients before serving.

Servings: 3

Soft Millet with Cauliflower

This dish looks and tastes very much like mashed potatoes.

> 4 cups water
> ½ tsp. sea salt
> 1 cup cauliflower (cut in flowerets)
> 1 cup millet (washed and drained)

1. Bring water to a boil. Add salt, cauliflower, and millet.
2. Cover and reduce flame. Simmer gently 40 minutes.

Servings: 4 or 5

Oat Pilaf

> ½ cup steel-cut oats
> ½ tsp. sea salt
> 3 Tbsp. carrot (cut in small cubes)
> 3 Tbsp. raisins
> 2 Tbsp. sunflower seeds
> 1¼ cups boiling water

1. Place first 5 ingredients in a saucepan.
2. Add the boiling water.
3. Bring to a second boil. Cover and simmer over very low flame 20 minutes.
4. Turn flame off and leave covered 5 minutes before serving.

Servings: 2

Quick Quinoa

> 2 cups water
> 1 cup quinoa (washed and drained)
> ¼ tsp. sea salt
> kernels cut from 2 ears cooked corn
> ½ bunch parsley (chopped)
> 4 Tbsp. sesame seeds (roasted)

1. Bring water to a boil.
2. Stir in quinoa and salt.
3. Reduce flame. Cover and simmer 15 minutes.
4. Stir in corn, parsley, and seeds just before serving.

Servings: 2

Herbed Quinoa

1 onion (chopped)
1 Tbsp. sesame oil
1¼ cup quinoa (washed and drained)
2½ cups water
1 tsp. natural soy sauce
½ tsp. dried rosemary
¼ tsp. sea salt
1 cup frozen green peas (thawed)
½ cup slivered almonds (roasted)

1. Sauté onion in oil about 5 minutes.
2. Add quinoa, water, soy sauce, rosemary, and salt.
3. Bring to a boil and lower flame. Cover and simmer 15 minutes.
4. Turn flame off and leave covered 5 minutes.
5. Stir in peas and almonds.
Servings: 3

Pressure-Cooked Kidney Beans and Spelt

Try substituting other beans and grains in this recipe. For example, wheat berries can be substituted for spelt.

1 Tbsp. sesame oil
½ onion (chopped)
½ cup kidney beans (washed and drained)
1½ cups whole spelt (washed and soaked 4 hours or overnight, in 4½ cups water)
¼ to ½ tsp. sea salt

1. Heat a pressure cooker over medium flame and add oil.
2. Sauté onion 2 to 3 minutes.
3. Add beans, spelt, and spelt soaking water. Bring to a boil and

fasten down the cover. Bring to pressure and cook over medium flame 1 hour.

4. Turn flame off. Allow pressure to come down naturally.
5. Add sea salt and simmer gently 15 minutes.

Servings: 6

Soba Noodle and Scallion "Pancake"=

Good served with steamed greens and a bowl of Lentil Barley Soup.

> **8 oz. soba noodles**
> **2 qts. boiling water**
> **1 bunch scallions (chopped)**
> **1 tsp. sesame oil**
> **1 Tbsp. natural soy sauce**
> **1½ Tbsp. sesame oil**
> **1½ Tbsp. toasted sesame oil**

1. Place noodles in a large pot of boiling water. Cook until tender.
2. Rinse noodles in cold water and drain.
3. In a mixing bowl, combine noodles, scallions, 1 teaspoon oil, and soy sauce.
4. Heat a heavy skillet. Add the remaining oils.
5. Add the noodle mixture and flatten slightly.
6. Cook over medium-low flame without stirring for 5 to 6 minutes or until noodles are light brown.
7. Turn "pancake" and cook the other side until light brown.
8. Using a spatula, remove to paper towel to drain before serving.

Servings: 2

Stir-Fried Noodles

1 Tbsp. toasted sesame oil
1 cup mushrooms (sliced)
1 cup scallions (sliced)
8 oz. udon noodles (cooked)
2 Tbsp. natural soy sauce
1 tsp. ginger juice (squeezed from grated fresh ginger root)
1 Tbsp. sesame seeds (lightly roasted)

1. Heat skillet and add oil. Add mushrooms and sauté for 1 minute over high flame.
2. Add scallions, noodles, soy sauce, and ginger juice. Sauté over high flame 1 or 2 minutes or until noodles are hot.
3. Sprinkle in sesame seeds and stir gently to mix.

Servings: 2 or 3

Vegetables

Of all the gifts of nature, none is better designed for human health than the rich variety of vegetables. Though vegetables are revered among traditional peoples, we in the West have only just begun to appreciate their benefits and mysteries. From a nutritional standpoint, the benefits of vegetables seem endless. They are the single greatest source of vitamins and minerals on earth. Take leafy greens, for example. A cup of cooked collard greens contains approximately 320 milligrams of calcium. That's more calcium than milk, which contains only about 300 milligrams per cup. Not only that, collard greens, as well as kale, mustard greens, cabbage, and broccoli, provide a wealth of other health-supporting nutrients, including many other minerals, vitamins, and fiber. And unlike milk, leafy greens contain no cholesterol, virtually no fat, and none of the antibiotics and steroids that are normally fed to cows.

Vegetables are health promoters. Collard greens, kale, mustard greens, broccoli, Brussels sprouts, and parsnips, as well as carrots, squash, and other yellow vegetables provide rich quantities of beta carotene, one of the most powerful immune boosters and cancer fighters one can eat. Beta carotene and vitamins C and E are called antioxidants, which inhibit the breakdown of atoms, molecules, and cells. Broccoli, cabbage, cauliflower, bell peppers, and squash all contain vitamin C. Most people don't realize it but broccoli and bell peppers, to name just two, provide richer quantities of vitamin C than citrus fruits.

Vitamin E can be found in whole grains. Many common vegetables provide iron, magnesium, zinc, potassium, manganese, and selenium, minerals which scientists tell us strengthen the immune system and are essential to healthy metabolism. Vegetables also contain what are now being called disease inhibitors. These nutrients, which have just begun to be studied and are still mysterious to scientists, actually prevent the onset and spread of illness. (See Meals That Heal, pages 199-205, for more information about nutrition and traditional approaches to health.)

Vegetables are rich sources of fiber, as well. Fiber maintains the health of the digestive tract, especially the colon. Studies have shown that fiber prevents intestinal disease, including colon cancer. Recent studies have shown that high-fiber diets are also linked with low rates of breast disease, including breast cancer.

Yet, there is much more to vegetables than their nutritive values. Within them lies the distillation of nature itself: the sun, captured and held by the plant's chlorophyll; the earth, drawn into the plant by its roots; rain, coursing through the plant's fibrous veins; and minerals which give the plant its upright nobility. Traditional medicine sees these natural characteristics as the basis for the plant's healing powers. For example, the Chinese maintain that the roots of a plant, which draw nutrients from the soil, are medicinal for the intestinal tract. Human intestines, say traditional Chinese healers, are the roots of the body, because they draw nutrients from our food, as the roots of the vegetables draw nutrients from the soil. Leafy greens, which fan out expansively, are seen as medicinal for the lungs, which work best when they, too, are open and unobstructed. Round vegetables, such as onions and squash, are seen as medicinal for the stomach and spleen. In fact, science has shown that onions protect against stomach cancer.

For millennia, traditional peoples from the Greeks to the Chinese, from the Asian Indians to the American Indians, have relied upon plants to treat disease and strengthen specific parts of the body.

Vegetables provide a rich assortment of tastes and textures — some crispy, others soft and luscious. When prepared correctly, vegetables provide a rainbow of tastes, textures, and colors. Vegetables are among the most colorful fruits of nature. Indeed, vegetables are art; delicious and nutritious art.

Tips for Cooking Vegetables

Don't overcook your vegetables. Leafy greens should be lightly to moderately steamed. Usually it takes only a few minutes to steam a pot of collard greens.

Learn to cook vegetables so that their integrity is maintained. Too much cooking destroys the vegetable and its taste. Also, use the cooking method that is appropriate for the vegetable. Bake squash to make it sweet; boil it to make it blend into the flavors of other vegetables and grains.

Vary your choice of vegetables among leafy green, round, and root vegetables, and try to eat a little of each every day. Rely on leafy greens for minerals, especially calcium.

Whenever possible, use organically grown vegetables, or vegetables grown without the use of artificial pesticides, herbicides, and fertilizers. Organic vegetables are nutritionally superior to conventionally grown produce. According to scientists at Rutgers University, who compared the nutritional contents of foods grown organically versus conventionally, organic vegetables contain far more calcium, magnesium, potassium, iron, and other nutrients. The Rutgers scientists found that organically grown cabbage, for example, contained 60 milligrams of calcium per hundred grams of cabbage, as compared to conventionally grown cabbage which contained only 17.5 milligrams of calcium per hundred grams. Organically grown lettuce contained 71 milligrams of calcium, while conventionally grown lettuce contained only 16 milligrams of calcium.

In addition to the nutrient content, artificial pesticides, herbicides, and other common farming additives have been shown to cause a wide range of disorders in people, including cancer and liver and kidney diseases.

Finally, treat all your vegetables with gratitude and respect. They are living things that will provide you with greater benefit than any of us fully understands.

Kale with Ume Dressing

Instead of Ume Dressing, I sometimes like to make a simple dressing by combining equal parts of umeboshi vinegar and extra-virgin olive oil.

> **1 bunch kale (washed and drained)**
> **2 cups boiling water**
> **1 Tbsp. sesame seeds (roasted)**
> **Ume Dressing**
> > **1 Tbsp. umeboshi paste**
> > **2 Tbsp. canola oil**
> > **1 Tbsp. lemon juice (freshly squeezed)**
> > **¾ cup orange juice (freshly squeezed)**
> > **3 Tbsp. raw tahini**

1. Place kale in boiling water and cook for 5 minutes over medium flame.
2. Drain kale and chop coarsely.
3. Blend all dressing ingredients in a blender.
4. Place kale in individual serving dishes. Drizzle about 2 teaspoons of dressing over each serving and garnish each serving with ½ teaspoon sesame seeds.

Servings: 4 or 5

Sesame Collards over Soba

> **1 bunch collard greens (washed and stems removed)**
> **2 cups boiling water**
> **4 Tbsp. sesame seeds (roasted)**
> **1 Tbsp. sesame oil**
> **2 cloves garlic (minced)**
> **2 tsp. natural soy sauce**
> **8 oz. soba noodles (cooked)**

1. Place collard greens in boiling water and cook for 5 minutes

over medium flame.

2. Drain and slice in $1/4$-inch strips.
3. Heat oil in skillet. Add minced garlic and collard greens. Sauté 2 to 3 minutes.
4. Season with soy sauce. Sprinkle sesame seeds over greens.
5. Place hot noodles in individual serving dishes and spoon collard greens over the noodles.

Servings: 4

Great Greens

Delicious with brown rice or udon noodles.

> **water**
> **1 bunch Chinese broccoli or Swiss chard**
> **Garlic Sauce**
> **3 Tbsp. sesame oil**
> **2 cloves garlic (sliced in thin rounds)**
> **3 Tbsp. natural soy sauce**

1. Bring 1 inch water to boil in a saucepan.
2. Place greens in boiling water. Simmer until tender, 3 to 5 minutes depending on type of green used.
3. Drain greens in a colander.
4. To make garlic sauce, heat a skillet and add oil and garlic. Sauté garlic over medium flame for a few seconds. (Be careful not to let it burn.)
5. Then, add soy sauce and turn flame off.
6. To serve, transfer greens to a serving dish and drizzle garlic sauce over.

Servings: 3 or 4

Steamed Greens

1 small bunch leafy greens, such as kale, collard greens, or turnip greens (cut in 1¹/₂-inch slices)
1 to 2 cups water

1. Place 1 or 2 inches of water in the bottom of pot. Place a steamer in the pot. Cover and bring to a boil.
2. Place the greens in the steamer basket. Cover and steam until tender but slightly crisp, about 5 to 7 minutes.

Servings: 3 or 4

Green Cabbage with Umeboshi Sauce

1¹/₂ cups water
2 cups green cabbage (thinly sliced)
2 tsp. umeboshi paste
2 tsp. kuzu, dissolved in 2 tsp. water

1. Bring water to a boil in a 2-quart saucepan. Add cabbage and boil 3 minutes.
2. Remove cabbage, reserving cooking water.
3. Add umeboshi paste to the reserved water and bring to a boil.
4. Stir in the dissolved kuzu and simmer briefly until sauce thickens.
5. Pour sauce over cabbage.

Servings: 3 or 4

Sweet and Sour Red Cabbage

Great served with tofu burgers or Chickpea Croquettes.

> **1 onion (minced)**
> **1 Tbsp. sesame oil**
> **4 Tbsp. maple syrup**
> **1/4 cup apple-cider vinegar**
> **1/2 tsp. sea salt**
> **1 small head red cabbage (shredded)**
> **3 tart apples (thinly sliced)**

1. Sauté onion in oil until tender.
2. Add maple syrup, vinegar, and salt. Stir to combine with onion.
3. Place remaining ingredients on top of onion mixture. Cover and simmer gently over low flame 25 to 30 minutes.
4. Stir to mix before serving.

Servings: 5 or 6

Red Cabbage and Apples in Raspberry Vinegar

This is a tasty side dish that can brighten up a bland meal.

> **1/2 cup water**
> **1/8 tsp. sea salt**
> **1 apple, any variety (chopped)**
> **2 cups red cabbage (chopped)**
> **1/4 cup raspberry vinegar**

1. In a saucepan, bring 1/2 cup water to boil.
2. Add salt, apple, and cabbage. Simmer gently 10 minutes, or until cabbage is wilted.
3. Stir in vinegar. Cover and simmer 10 minutes longer.

Servings: 4

Sautéed Cabbage and Carrots

> 2 tsp. toasted sesame oil
> 1 cup green cabbage (thinly sliced)
> 1/8 tsp. sea salt
> 1 cup carrots (cut in matchsticks)
> 1 tsp. sesame seeds (lightly roasted)

1. Heat a skillet. Add oil, cabbage, and salt.
2. Sauté cabbage for 2 minutes over high flame.
3. Add carrots and sauté 4 minutes longer, stirring constantly.
4. Sprinkle with sesame seeds before serving.

Servings: 3 or 4

Quick Boiled Vegetables

These vegetables can be mixed and served plain or with a salad dressing, or garnished with roasted pumpkin seeds.

> 2 cups water
> 1/2 cup carrots (thinly sliced on diagonal)
> 2 cups kale (sliced)
> 1 cup green cabbage (sliced in small squares)

1. Place water in a saucepan and bring to a boil.
2. Add carrots and boil 1 or 2 minutes.
3. Remove carrots. Drain and place in a bowl to cool.
4. Add kale to the same boiling water and boil 2 or 3 minutes.
5. Remove kale. Drain and add to the bowl with the carrots.
6. Add the cabbage to the boiling water and boil 1 or 2 minutes.
7. Remove cabbage. Drain and place cabbage in bowl with carrots and kale.

Servings: 5 or 6

Shredded Carrot with Orange Zest

A light side dish with a heavy meal. Refreshing and flavorful, it cleanses the palate.

> **3 cups carrots (shredded)**
> **pinch sea salt**
> **1/2 tsp. grated orange rind**
> **4 Tbsp. water**
> **1/2 apple (seeds removed)**

1. Preheat oven to 350 degrees.
2. Heap shredded carrots loosely in a baking dish. Add salt and orange rind.
3. Sprinkle water over carrots. Place apple, cut side down, on top.
4. Cover and bake at 350 for 15 or 20 minutes.
5. Discard apple before serving.

Servings: 3 or 4

Carrots in Orange Juice

> **2/3 cup orange juice (freshly squeezed)**
> **1 tsp. arrowroot**
> **3 cups carrots (sliced)**
> **1/4 tsp. cinnamon**

1. Combine juice and arrowroot in saucepan. Add carrots and cinnamon.
2. Cover and cook over low flame 15 to 20 minutes or until carrots are tender.

Servings: 3 or 4

Sunshine Carrots

4 carrots (cut in 2-inch lengths)
2 cups water
¼ tsp. sea salt
2 tsp. barley malt
1 tsp. arrowroot
¼ tsp. sea salt
¼ tsp. ground ginger
¼ cup orange juice (freshly squeezed)

1. Place carrots, water, and salt in a saucepan. Cook 15 to 20 minutes or until just tender. Drain.
2. Combine remaining ingredients in a small saucepan. Cook over low heat, stirring constantly.
3. Pour over carrots. Stir gently until carrots are well coated.

Servings: 3 or 4

Kinpira

1 Tbsp. sesame oil
2 fresh burdock roots (cut in matchsticks)
2 carrots (cut in matchsticks)
½ cup water, approximately
½ to 1 tsp. natural soy sauce

1. Heat pan and add oil. Add burdock and sauté about 10 minutes.
2. Add carrot and sauté another 10 minutes.
3. Add enough water to almost cover the vegetables. Cover and simmer 20 minutes.
4. Season with soy sauce.
5. Simmer another 20 minutes or until vegetables are tender.

Servings: 5

Matchstick Turnips with Sesame Seeds

3 cups water
¼ tsp. sea salt
2 cups turnips (cut in matchsticks)
1 Tbsp. sesame oil
1 Tbsp. sesame seeds
1 Tbsp. parsley (chopped)
⅛ tsp. sea salt

1. Place water and ¼ teaspoon salt in a saucepan and bring to a boil.
2. Quick-boil turnips for 1 minute and drain.
3. Heat a skillet. Add oil and sauté sesame seeds until golden.
4. Add turnips. Season with salt and sprinkle with parsley.
5. Stir until turnips are heated through.

Servings: 3 or 4

Pan-Roasted Vegetables

3 cups cauliflower (cut into flowerets)
2 cups carrots (cut in strips)
2 onions (quartered)
2 rutabagas (cut in strips)
½ cup water

1. Preheat oven to 400 degrees.
2. Place vegetables in an oiled baking pan.
3. Add water. Cover and bake at 400 degrees for 30 minutes or until vegetables are tender.

Servings: 6

Nishime-Style Vegetables

1 carrot
½ rutabaga
¼ head cabbage
1 strip kombu, 4 inches long and 1 inch wide (soaked in
    water to cover)
2 tsp. natural soy sauce
water

1. Cut vegetables in 2-inch chunks or wedges.
2. Drain kombu and reserve soaking water. Cut kombu in 1-inch-square pieces.
3. Place kombu in the bottom of a heavy pot. Add soaking water.
4. Layer carrots, rutabaga, and cabbage over kombu. Sprinkle soy sauce over the vegetables.
5. Add additional water to reach a depth of ½ inch.
6. Cover and cook over high flame until water begins to boil.
7. Lower flame and cook gently for about 20 minutes, or until vegetables are tender.

Servings: 4

Maple-Glazed Pea Pods and Carrots

¾ cup water
2 cups carrots (sliced)
8 oz. snow peas (strings removed)
3 Tbsp. sesame oil
½ tsp. arrowroot
2 Tbsp. maple syrup

1. In a small saucepan, bring water to a boil.
2. Add carrots. Cover and cook just until tender.
3. Add snow peas. Continue cooking one minute.

4. Immediately drain vegetables in a colander. Set aside.
5. Heat pan and add sesame oil.
6. With a wire whisk, stir in arrowroot and maple syrup.
7. Using a wooden spoon, gently stir in carrots and snow peas. Heat through.

Servings: 4

Lima Beans and Scallions

Great served over noodles or whole grain.

> **3 cups frozen lima beans**
> **5 scallions (thinly sliced)**
> **3 Tbsp. sesame oil**
> **1 Tbsp. unbleached flour or whole-wheat pastry flour**
> **$^3/_4$ tsp. sea salt**

1. Cook beans according to package instructions. Drain, reserving $^1/_2$ cup liquid.
2. Sauté scallions in oil.
3. Add flour, stirring until smooth. Cook 1 minute more, stirring constantly.
4. Gradually stir in the $^1/_2$ cup reserved cooking liquid. Add salt. Cook until thickened, about 2 minutes.
5. Stir in lima beans.

Servings: 6

Green Beans Almondine

3 cups water
1/2 tsp. sea salt
1 1/2 cups green beans (tips removed)
2 Tbsp. sesame oil
1/4 cup slivered almonds
2 Tbsp. parsley (chopped)

1. Bring water to a boil in a saucepan.
2. Add salt and cook beans for 5 minutes.
3. Drain beans.
4. Heat a skillet over medium flame and add sesame oil. Add almonds and sauté 3 minutes.
5. Add green beans and parsley. Stir to heat through.

Servings: 4 or 5

String Beans with Almonds

25 to 30 fresh string beans (strings removed)
3 cups boiling water
10 almonds (chopped)
2 tsp. sesame oil
2 cloves garlic (minced)
1/4 tsp. sea salt

1. Place beans in boiling water and cook for 5 minutes.
2. Drain beans and set aside.
3. Preheat skillet over medium flame. Place almonds in skillet and stir until lightly roasted.
4. Remove almonds from skillet and set aside.
5. Heat oil in skillet and add garlic, string beans, and salt. Stir-fry for 3 minutes.
6. Add almonds. Stir before serving.

Servings: 3

Leek Sauté

Delicious served over grain or pasta.

> 3 Tbsp. sesame oil
> 3 carrots (sliced)
> 3 ribs celery (sliced)
> 2 large leeks (sliced)
> 1 onion (chopped)
> $1/2$ tsp. sea salt
> 1 cup mushrooms (sliced)
> 3 Tbsp. parsley (chopped)
> 1 tsp. dried dillweed

1. Heat a large skillet and add oil.
2. Add carrots and sauté 2 minutes. Reduce flame to low.
3 Add celery, leeks, onion, and salt. Sauté until vegetables are tender, about 10 minutes.
4. Add mushrooms, parsley, and dillweed. Cover and simmer 5 minutes.

Servings: 5 or 6

Herbed Jerusalem Artichokes

> 4 Jerusalem artichokes (peeled)
> 3 Tbsp. sesame oil
> 2 tsp. dried sage (rubbed)
> 2 Tbsp. lemon juice (freshly squeezed)
> $1/8$ tsp. sea salt

1. Steam artichokes until tender, about 20 minutes.
2. Cut artichokes into slices.
3. Heat skillet and add sesame oil. Add sage and sauté briefly.
4. Add artichoke slices and cook until heated through.
5. Sprinkle with lemon juice and season with salt to taste.

Servings: 4

Quick Skillet Corn

kernels cut from 4 ears corn
2 Tbsp. sesame oil
$\frac{1}{4}$ tsp. sea salt
3 scallions (thinly sliced)
3 Tbsp. green bell pepper (minced)
3 Tbsp. parsley (minced)

1. Sauté corn in oil over medium flame about 2 minutes.
2. Add salt, scallions, and bell pepper. Cook 2 minutes.
3. Stir in parsley before serving.
Servings: 3

Scalloped Cauliflower

4 cups cooked cauliflower flowerets
$2\frac{1}{2}$ cups White Sauce, page 153 (double recipe)
$\frac{1}{4}$ to $\frac{1}{2}$ cup bread crumbs

1. Preheat oven to 350 degrees.
2. Place a layer of half the cooked cauliflower in an oiled 9-inch-square casserole dish. Cover with half the white sauce.
3. Add a second layer of cauliflower and the remaining white sauce. Top with bread crumbs.
4. Bake uncovered at 350 degrees for 30 to 45 minutes.
Servings: 4 to 5

Cauliflower au Gratin

1 head cauliflower (cut into flowerets)
1½ Tbsp. Dijon-style mustard
1 Tbsp. apple-juice concentrate
¼ to ½ cup whole-wheat bread crumbs

1. Steam cauliflower until tender.
2. Preheat oven to 350 degrees.
3. Place cauliflower in an oiled baking dish.
4. Combine mustard and juice. Spread over top of cauliflower. Sprinkle bread crumbs on top.
5. Bake uncovered at 350 degrees 15 to 20 minutes.

Servings: 4 or 5

Sesame Broccoli

1 Tbsp. sesame oil
2 Tbsp. natural soy sauce
4 cups broccoli (cut into flowerets)
1 Tbsp. sesame seeds (roasted)

1. Heat oil and soy sauce in large saucepan.
2. Add broccoli. Stir-fry over medium-high flame for 5 minutes, adding 1 to 2 tablespoons water if needed.
3. Cover and reduce heat. Simmer gently for 1 minute.
4. Garnish with sesame seeds.

Servings: 4 or 5

Chinese Stir-Fry

Delicious served over brown rice or whole-grain pasta.

> 2 Tbsp. sesame oil
> 1 Tbsp. ginger root (minced)
> 2 lbs. vegetables (sliced or cut appropriately for stir-fry):
>   use any combination of onions, carrots, broccoli, and
>   cabbage
> 1/4 tsp. sea salt
> 2 or 3 Tbsp. water
> 1 tsp. maple syrup
> 1 tsp. mirin
> 1 Tbsp. natural soy sauce
> 4 scallions (sliced)

1. Heat large skillet or wok over high flame.
2. Add oil and ginger. Cook 20 to 30 seconds.
3. Add onions, if used, and stir briefly.
4. Add remaining vegetables and salt. Stir-fry 1 minute to coat
   vegetables with oil.
5. Combine water, maple syrup, mirin, and soy sauce in a separate bowl.
6. Add this mixture to the stir-fry. Cover and cook over medium-high flame 1 to 2 minutes.
7. Remove cover and stir in scallions before serving.

Servings: 4 or 5

Scalloped Squash

Loaded with Vitamin A. Tasty and strengthening. A nice dish
to take to a pot-luck.

> 4 cups butternut squash (thinly sliced)
> 5 onions (chopped and sautéed until transparent)
> 1 cup almonds

2 cups boiling water
4 cups water
1 tsp. sea salt
¼ cup whole-wheat pastry flour

1. Preheat oven to 350 degrees.
2. In an oiled baking dish, alternate layers of squash and sautéed onions.
3. Place almonds in boiling water for 2 minutes to loosen skins.
4. Discard skins and water.
5. In a blender, purée almonds with 4 cups water, salt, and flour.
6. Transfer to a saucepan and bring to a boil.
7. Pour almond purée over squash and onions.
8. Cover baking dish and bake at 350 degrees 30 minutes or until squash is tender.

Servings: 6

Fiesta Squash

2 Tbsp. sesame oil
1 medium onion (chopped)
1 green pepper (chopped)
1½ lbs. yellow squash (sliced)
½ tsp. sea salt
1 tsp. lemon juice (freshly squeezed)

1. Heat a skillet and add oil. Sauté onion and green pepper until tender.
2. Stir in remaining ingredients. Cover and cook over low heat 10 minutes or until squash is just tender.

Servings: 2

Holiday Acorn Squash

2 medium acorn squash
½ cup water
3 Tbsp. corn oil
3 Tbsp. maple syrup or barley malt
¼ tsp. cinnamon
2 tsp. vanilla extract
⅓ cup pecans (chopped)

1. Preheat oven to 350 degrees.
2. Cut each squash in half and remove seeds.
3. Place squash halves in baking dish, cut sides up. Pour water into baking dish.
4. Combine remaining ingredients and place in squash cavities.
5. Cover and bake at 350 degrees approximately 35 minutes or until tender.

Servings: 4

Maple Acorn Squash

1 acorn squash
1 tsp. corn oil
2 Tbsp. maple syrup

1. Preheat oven to 350 degrees.
2. Cut squash in half and remove seeds.
3. Place squash halves in a baking dish, cut sides up.
4. Combine oil with syrup and spoon equally into cavities of squash.
5. Cover and bake at 350 degrees 35 to 40 minutes or until tender.

Servings: 2

Dried Daikon and Kombu

**1 strip kombu, 4 inches long and 1 inch wide (soaked 5
 minutes and thinly sliced)**
**2 cups dried daikon (rinsed, soaked 10 minutes in water
 to cover, and drained)**
1 to 2 cups water
1 Tbsp. natural soy sauce

1. Place the kombu in a saucepan and place the daikon on top.
 Add enough water to cover the daikon.
2. Cover and bring to a boil over medium-high flame. Reduce
 the flame to medium low. Simmer about 35 minutes, or until
 the kombu is tender.
3. Add soy sauce and continue to simmer uncovered until all
 liquid has cooked off.

Servings: 4 or 5

Saucy Sauerkraut

2 tsp. sesame oil
1 cup onions (chopped)
1 cup natural sauerkraut
¼ cup apple juice
½ tsp. caraway seeds

1. Heat skillet and add oil. Add onions and sauté until transparent.
2. Add remaining ingredients and heat through.

Servings: 3

Beans

I love beans. They're rich, hearty, and stick-to-your-ribs filling. Beans contain more protein and fat than grains and vegetables and are therefore more luscious. They round out the meal, giving it another set of flavors and a satisfying weight and texture. Beans are great with any grain and they are especially wonderful with corn bread.

Beans are more acidic than grains, the result of their higher protein content. Therefore, they should be cooked with kombu seaweed, which helps alkalize the beans and makes them easier to digest. This requires no more effort than placing a small piece of kombu into the pot of beans and water. The seaweed is virtually tasteless. It will dissolve during the cooking and in the process, will soften the beans and add many minerals and vitamins that enhance the body's immune system.

Beans are highly nutritious. According to the U.S. Department of Agriculture's *Composition of Foods, Handbook No. 8*, beans and bean products are rich sources of protein, carbohydrates, vitamin A, B vitamins, niacin, phosphorus, and fiber.

There is a wide variety of tastes and textures among beans. Here is a list of the most common beans available today: azuki, black-eyed peas, black soybeans, chickpeas, great northern beans, kidney beans, lima beans, lentils, navy beans, pinto beans, soybeans, and split peas.

An assortment of high-quality processed foods is derived from beans, as well, including tempeh, tofu, natto, miso, and soy sauce. Except for tofu, all of these are fermented foods.

Tempeh is fermented soybeans that remain essentially whole but are combined in a patty. It can be cut up in squares and added to soups, noodle broths, or fried in a little sesame oil until brown and crispy. Delicious, especially with brown rice and stir-fried vegetables, tempeh also can be used as a burger to make sandwiches.

Tofu, also made from soybeans, is a more refined food. Rich in calcium, tofu is wonderful in soups, broths, or as a side dish with a little soy sauce and freshly grated ginger root.

Natto, made from fermented soybeans, serves as a condiment with grains, noodles, or vegetables. Like tempeh, miso, and soy sauce, natto is rich in digestive enzymes and friendly bacteria.

Miso, one of the most delicious fermented bean products, is a combination of naturally aged and processed soybeans and grain. It comes as a paste and serves as a stock for soups, broths, stews, and noodle broths. Miso contains lecithin and has been shown to break down fats in the digestive tract, thus reducing fat and cholesterol in the blood stream. Miso helps alkalize the blood and restores friendly bacteria to the intestines.

Naturally aged and processed soy sauce is delicious, especially when added to soups, broths, sauces, and dressings.

Tips for Preparing Beans

Most beans require an hour and a half of cooking time, but they're worth it. However, you can have a bean dish on the table in a lot less time. As with grain, there are slower- and faster-cooking beans. Let's look first at how to speed up the cooking time for the slow-cooking variety. The first thing to do is presoak the beans in cold water overnight or four to five hours before cooking. Second, cook the beans with a strip of kombu seaweed as described above. (Carrot and onion will also help alkalize the beans and are delicious when added with the kombu.) Don't season your beans with sea salt until they are at least 80 percent done; otherwise, they will never become properly soft.

Now, let's look at some of the faster-cooking beans. The quickest beans of all are red lentils, which take no more than twenty-five minutes to cook. Next, green and yellow split peas, which require half an hour. Green or brown lentils take thirty to forty minutes.

As for the processed beans, tempeh can be steamed, fried, deep-fried, boiled, sautéed, or stewed. It's fast and delicious. Tofu can be steamed, fried, or boiled in less than twenty minutes. Natto is nice served in miso soup or over rice as a condiment.

Anyway you cook or slice it, beans are a healthful and wonderful addition to your meal.

Anasazi Beans with Kombu ══════

2 cups anasazi beans (washed and drained)
water to cover
1 strip kombu, 4 inches long and 1 inch wide
1 onion (chopped and sautéed), optional
1 carrot (diced), optional
$\frac{1}{2}$ tsp. sea salt

1. Soak beans in water to cover overnight.
2. Drain beans and add fresh water to cover.
3. Add kombu and onions, if using. Cover and simmer about $1\frac{1}{2}$ hours or until beans are tender.
4. Add carrots, if using, and season with salt. Cover and simmer 10 minutes longer.

Servings: 6 to 8

Basic Azuki Beans

I have found it unnecessary to soak azuki beans as they seem to cook up more tender without soaking. This is a simple recipe and very delicious served with a garnish of raw scallions.

1 cup azuki beans (washed and drained)
4½ cups water
1 strip kombu, 3 inches long and 1 inch wide
1 tsp. natural soy sauce

1. Place beans, water, and kombu in a saucepan. Cover and bring to a boil.
2. Reduce flame and simmer 1¼ hour, stirring occasionally. Add more water as needed.
3. When beans are tender, add soy sauce. Simmer 10 to 15 minutes longer

Servings: 4

Azuki Squash Kombu

1 cup azuki beans (washed and drained)
1 strip kombu, 4 inches long and 1 inch wide
4½ cups water
1½ cups butternut squash (peeled and cubed)
1 tsp. natural soy sauce, or ½ tsp. sea salt

1. Place beans in a saucepan with kombu and water.
2. Bring to a boil and lower flame. Cover and simmer about 1¼ hours, adding a little water only if needed.
3. Add squash. Cover and continue to simmer until squash is soft.
4. Season with soy sauce or salt. Simmer 2 to 3 minutes.

Servings: 3 or 4

Good Old Black-Eyed Peas

In the Southern tradition, eating black-eyed peas on New Year's Day is supposed to bring good luck for the rest of the year. For a different taste, I sometimes add a dash of thyme along with the salt.

> **2 cups black-eyed peas (washed and soaked overnight in water to cover)**
> **1 cup onion (chopped)**
> **8 cups fresh water**
> **3 cloves garlic (minced)**
> **1 jalapeño pepper (seeded and chopped)**
> **1½ tsp. sea salt, or to taste**

1. Drain peas and discard the soaking water.
2. Bring peas, onions, and fresh water to a boil.
3. Lower flame. Cover and simmer about 40 minutes.
4. Add garlic and jalapeño pepper. Cover and simmer about 20 minutes.
5. Season with salt. Simmer a few minutes longer.

Servings: 6 to 8

Black-Eyed Peas with Sassafras

My mother used to send me to school with corn bread and a jar of black-eyed peas with sassafras. These are still among my favorite beans. I used to get mad at her because the other kids had peanut butter and jelly sandwiches. Now I'm grateful.

> **1 cup black-eyed peas (washed and drained)**
> **4 cups water**
> **1 strip kombu, 4 inches long and 1 inch wide**
> **1 bay leaf**
> **1 onion (chopped)**
> **1 clove garlic (minced)**

1 carrot (chopped)
1 rib celery (thinly sliced)
$\frac{1}{2}$ tsp. sassafras powder
$\frac{1}{2}$ tsp. dried thyme
$\frac{1}{8}$ tsp. poultry seasoning
1 tsp. sea salt

1. Combine peas, water, kombu, and bay leaf in a pot. Bring to a boil and lower flame. Cover and simmer approximately 50 minutes.
2. Lightly oil a skillet and sauté onion 5 minutes.
3. Add garlic, carrot, and celery and sauté another 3 minutes.
4. Add sassafras, thyme, and poultry seasoning to vegetables in the skillet and combine very well.
5. Stir the skillet mixture into the soup pot and add salt to taste. Simmer 10 to 15 minutes to combine the flavors.

Servings: 3 or 4

Chickpeas with Kombu

2 cups chickpeas (washed and soaked 6 to 8 hours)
2 strips kombu, 6 to 8 inches long and 1 inch wide
(soaked 3 to 5 minutes and diced)
6 cups fresh water, approximately
$\frac{3}{4}$ tsp. sea salt

1. Drain the chickpeas and discard the soaking water.
2. Place the kombu in the bottom of a heavy cooking pot.
3. Set the chickpeas on top. Add water just to cover the chickpeas. Cover and bring to a boil.
4. Reduce the flame to medium low and simmer about $2\frac{1}{2}$ to 3 hours.
5. When the chickpeas are tender, season with salt. Simmer another 15 minutes.

Servings: 8

Kidney Beans with Miso

2 cups kidney beans (washed and soaked
overnight in water to cover)
1 strip kombu, 4 inches long and 1 inch wide
fresh water to cover
2 onions (chopped and sautéed)
¼ tsp. sea salt
1 tsp. brown-rice miso

1. Drain beans and discard soaking water.
2. Place beans and kombu in a pot with fresh water to cover.
3. Bring to a boil and reduce flame. Cover and simmer about
   1 hour or until beans are tender.
4. Add onions, salt, and miso. Simmer gently 15 minutes.
Servings: 6 to 8

Lentils with Kombu and Onions

2 strips kombu, 6 to 8 inches long and 1 inch wide
(soaked 3 to 5 minutes and diced)
2 cups onions (sliced in thick half moons)
2 cups green lentils (washed and drained)
6 cups water
¾ tsp. sea salt
2 scallions (thinly sliced)

1. Place the kombu and onions in a pot. Add lentils and water.
   Cover and bring to a boil.
2. Reduce the flame to medium low and simmer 25 minutes, or
   until lentils are about 80-percent done.
3. Season with salt. Cover and cook another 15 to 20 minutes.
4. Place in a serving bowl and garnish with scallions.
Servings: 8

Lentils with Spinach

2 Tbsp. sesame oil
1 clove garlic (minced)
1 shallot (minced)
4 cups spinach (coarsely chopped)
2 cups cooked green lentils (cooked al dente)
$\frac{1}{2}$ tsp. sea salt

1. Heat skillet over medium flame and add oil.
2. Sauté garlic and shallot 1 minute.
3. Add spinach and lentils. Season with salt. Stir and cook until spinach wilts.

Servings: 6

Lentils 'n Wheat Fixins

Here's a great one-pot dish that is sure to please. Leftovers can be transferred while still hot to an eight-inch baking dish. Next day, slice, heat, and serve with Onion Gravy.

$\frac{1}{2}$ cup brown lentils (washed and drained)
3 cups water
2 onions (chopped and sautéed until transparent)
$\frac{3}{4}$ cup bulgur
2 tsp. sea salt
2 tsp. granulated onion
$\frac{1}{2}$ tsp. granulated garlic

1. Place lentils and water in saucepan. Cover and bring to a boil.
2. Add onions. Cover and simmer 25 minutes.
3. Add bulgur, salt, and granulated onion and garlic. Cover and simmer 20 minutes longer.
4. Turn off flame and leave covered 5 minutes before serving.

Servings: 6

Herbed Lentils and Carrots

2 Tbsp. olive oil
1 onion (chopped)
2 carrots (sliced in rounds)
2 cloves garlic (minced)
1 cup green lentils (washed and drained)
3 cups vegetable stock or water
$\frac{1}{2}$ to 1 tsp. sea salt
1 tsp. dried marjoram

1. Heat a heavy saucepan over medium flame and add oil.
2. Add onion and sauté until soft.
3. Add carrots and garlic and cook 2 minutes.
4. Add lentils and stock or water. Cover and bring to a boil.
5. Reduce flame and simmer gently about 30 minutes or until lentils are tender and most of the liquid is absorbed.
6. Season with salt and simmer 15 minutes. Simmer uncovered if necessary to evaporate liquid.
7. Mix in marjoram.

Servings: 3 or 4

Lentil Stew

4 cups water
1 cup lentils (washed and drained)
1 strip kombu, 3 inches long and 1 inch wide
1 onion (diced)
1 rib celery (thinly sliced)
1 tsp. sea salt
1 carrot (cubed)

1. Place water, lentils, kombu, onion, and celery in saucepan. Cover and bring to a boil.
2. Reduce flame. Simmer for 45 minutes.
3. Add salt and carrot. Simmer 10 to 15 minutes.

Servings: 4 or 5

Beans in Sweet Mustard Sauce

Try this for a change of pace in your bean cuisine.

1 cup navy beans (washed and soaked 4 hours or overnight in water to cover)
4 cups fresh water
1 tsp. sea salt
2 tsp. dry mustard
2 tsp. maple syrup
2 tsp. lemon juice (freshly squeezed)

1. Drain beans and discard soaking water.
2. Place beans in pot with fresh water. Cover and cook 1½ to 2 hours until tender.
3. Drain beans, reserving ½ cup of liquid.
4. Combine the ½ cup liquid with salt, mustard, maple syrup, and lemon juice. Pour over the beans. Bring to a boil and simmer 3 minutes.

Servings: 3 or 4

Quick Vegetarian Chili

I serve this chili over udon noodles or brown rice.

> **1 onion (chopped)**
> **2 ribs celery (thinly sliced)**
> **2 carrots (chopped)**
> **2 Tbsp. corn oil**
> **6½ oz. vegetarian chili mix**
> **8 cups water**
> **3 cups cooked pinto beans**
> **1 tsp. cumin**
> **1 tsp. chili powder, optional**

1. Sauté onion, celery, and carrots in oil.
2. Add chili mix and water. Cover and simmer 15 minutes.
3. Add pinto beans and cumin. Cover and simmer 10 to 15 minutes longer.
4. Taste and add chili powder if desired.

Servings: 6

Refried Beans

I like to serve this as a side dish with rice or garnished with scallions and rolled in corn tortillas.

> **4 cups pinto beans (washed and soaked overnight)**
> **10 to 12 cups fresh water**
> **2 cups onions (chopped)**
> **2 cloves garlic (minced)**
> **1 Tbsp. cumin**
> **½ tsp. dried oregano**
> **2 tsp. sea salt**

1. Drain beans and discard the soaking water.
2. Add fresh water and bring to a full boil.
3. Add onions. Reduce flame. Cover and cook about 1 hour or until beans are soft.
4. Season with garlic, cumin, oregano, and salt. Simmer uncovered 20 minutes to cook off most of the liquid.
5. Drain beans if any liquid remains, and mash. Adjust seasoning.

Servings: 12 to 14

Sea Vegetables

When it comes to seaweed, you should know first of all that it is among the most important foods you can eat. It's loaded with immune-strengthening vitamins and minerals. Research has shown that it can actually leach heavy metals and radioactive particles from the tissues of your body.

But in order to eat it, you have to learn how to prepare it so you can enjoy its flavor. We served seaweed every day in my restaurant. Now you might think that Texans would hate seaweed, but my customers came to love it. One of their favorites was arame, which is also one of the most nutritious foods on the planet. Here's how I prepare it: First, I wash the arame by placing it in a big mixing bowl and swishing it around to loosen any dirt. Then I lift the arame out of the bowl, thus lifting it from the dirt in the water, and place it into a colander. I let the arame drain. Meanwhile, I sauté some chopped onions in toasted sesame oil in a saucepan (five minutes is all they need). Then I layer the arame on top of the onions and pour water down the sides of the pan until it reaches a point just below the top of the arame. I bring the mix to a rapid boil over high flame. Once the arame boils, I lower the flame, cover the pan, and gently simmer for 35 to 40 minutes. Afterwards, I season with soy sauce, and then cook an additional two to three minutes. Now it's ready to serve.

Lemon and sesame seeds can be added to any seaweed to make a nice garnish. Try combining cooked arame with sauerkraut. Hijiki is wonderful sautéed with garlic and ginger and simmered for 45 minutes. You can turn hijiki into a delicious salad by adding raw or lightly steamed vegetables and a vinaigrette dressing. Sea palm requires pre-soaking and is great sautéed with garlic and sesame oil. Finally, toasted sushi nori is ready to eat. Just take sushi nori out of the package and wrap some rice in it.

Now, for a little information about seaweeds. First, sea vegetables bring us the life-giving powers of the oceans. Among the
many nutrients they contain is sodium alginate. Scientists at
McGill University in Montreal have discovered that sodium alginate binds with chemical pollutants, heavy metals, and radioactive particles, thus allowing these elements to be eliminated
from the body via the digestive tract.

Seaweeds also provide rich quantities of beta carotene, B vitamins, vitamin C, calcium, zinc, phosphorus, potassium, magnesium, and other minerals. We need these immune-enhancing
and cleansing foods because our environment is loaded with
pollutants.

Sea vegetables can be prepared in so many delicious ways
that after you have learned to prepare them properly you can
stop thinking about their nutritional benefits and eat them for
the pleasure of your palate alone.

Arame Sauté

1 Tbsp. toasted sesame oil
1 onion (finely diced)
1 cup arame (washed and drained)
 water to cover
1 Tbsp. natural soy sauce

1. Heat saucepan. Add oil and onion.
2. Layer washed arame over onion. Add enough water to come
   just below the top of the arame.
3. Bring to a boil and reduce flame. Cover and simmer 20 minutes.
4. Sprinkle soy sauce over arame. Simmer 10 minutes longer.
5. Taste and adjust seasoning.
Servings: 5

Arame with Carrots and Onions

1/2 cup water
2 cups onions (cut in crescents)
2 cups carrots (cut in matchsticks)
2 cups arame (washed and drained)
water to cover
2 to 3 tsp. soy sauce

1. Place 1/2 cup water in a skillet and bring to a boil.
2. Add the onions and water-sauté for about 2 to 3 minutes.
3. Add the carrots and sauté 2 minutes.
4. Set the arame on top of the onions and carrots. Add water to cover just the vegetables, not the arame. Add 1/2 teaspoon of soy sauce. Bring to a boil.
5. Reduce the flame to medium low. Cover and simmer for 35 to 40 minutes. Season with remaining soy sauce.
6. Cook uncovered until almost all liquid has evaporated. Mix and place in a serving bowl.

Servings: 10

Hijiki with Ume Dressing

1 cup hijiki (washed and soaked 1 hour)
3 cups water
2 tsp. natural soy sauce
Ume Dressing
1/2 cup sesame seeds (lightly roasted)
3 Tbsp. umeboshi vinegar
1/4 cup parsley (chopped)
1 Tbsp. lemon juice (freshly squeezed)
1/2 cup water

1. Drain hijiki and place in a saucepan with fresh water to cover.

2. Bring to a boil and add soy sauce. Reduce flame. Cover and simmer 30 minutes.
3. Drain hijiki and let cool while preparing dressing.
4. Place dressing ingredients in a blender and blend until smooth.
5. Pour the dressing over the hijiki and mix well.

Servings: 6 to 8

Hijiki with Lotus Root and Onions

½ cup hijiki
½ cup water
1 cup onions (cut in thin lengthwise crescents)
1 cup lotus root (cut in thin half-rounds)
water to cover
1½ tsp. natural soy sauce

1. Rinse and soak hijiki in water to cover for 30 minutes. Drain.
2. Place ½ cup water in a skillet and bring to a boil. Add the onions and water-sauté for about 2 minutes.
3. Add the lotus root and sauté for 2 minutes.
4. Set the hijiki on top of the onions and lotus root. Do not mix in.
5. Add water to cover just the vegetables, not the hijiki. Add ½ teaspoon soy sauce.
6. Cover and bring to a boil. Reduce the flame to medium low and simmer 40 minutes.
7. Add water occasionally, if necessary, but only to almost cover the vegetables each time.
8. Season with remaining soy sauce. Simmer until almost all remaining liquid is gone.

Servings: 5 or 6

Hijiki Onion Sauté

For best results this dish should be cooked in a heavy, cast-iron pot with a heavy tight-fitting lid.

> $\frac{1}{2}$ oz. hijiki
> $1\frac{1}{2}$ cups water, for soaking
> 1 Tbsp. toasted sesame oil
> 3 onions (coarsely chopped)
> $\frac{1}{8}$ tsp. sea salt
> 1 Tbsp. natural soy sauce

1. Wash hijiki. Soak in water for 30 minutes.
2. Drain hijiki and discard soaking water.
3. Heat oil in a heavy pot. Add onions.
4. Sprinkle salt over onions. Cover and cook 10 minutes over medium-low flame until onions release their own juices.
5. Layer hijiki over onions and sprinkle with soy sauce. Reduce flame and place pot on preheated heat diffuser. Cover and cook gently 35 to 40 minutes.
6. Stir before serving.

Servings: 4

Hijiki Sauté

Try serving this dish with a garnish of sesame seeds or roasted pumpkin seeds.

> $\frac{1}{2}$ cup hijiki
> 1 Tbsp. toasted sesame oil
> water to cover
> 2 tsp. natural soy sauce

1. Rinse and soak hijiki in water for 30 minutes. Drain hijiki.
2. Heat a skillet and add oil. Sauté hijiki 5 minutes.
3. Add enough water to almost cover the hijiki. Cover and simmer gently 40 minutes.

4. Season with soy sauce and simmer a few minutes, uncovered, until most of the liquid has cooked off.

Servings: 4

Pressure-Cooked Kombu

Great served as a side dish with brown rice.

>**3 strips kombu, 4 inches long and 1 inch wide**
>**2$^1/_2$ cups water**
>**1 Tbsp. natural soy sauce**

1. Place ingredients in a pressure cooker.
2. Lock lid on cooker and bring to pressure.
3. Reduce flame and simmer gently 30 minutes.
4. Turn flame off. Allow pressure to drop naturally.

Servings: 3

Wonderful Wakame

For a nice variation, try replacing the ginger juice with two tablespoons brown-rice vinegar.

>**3 strips wakame, about 6 inches long and 1 inch wide**
>**water to cover**
>**2 Tbsp. natural soy sauce**
>**1 tsp. ginger juice (squeezed from grated fresh ginger root)**

1. Soak wakame in water to cover for 30 minutes.
2. Drain wakame and cut in small slices.
3. Simmer wakame in fresh water to cover until tender, about 20 minutes.
4. Drain water off, leaving wakame in saucepan.
5. Combine soy sauce and fresh ginger juice. Pour over wakame and simmer 1 minute.

Servings: 4

Sea Palm Sauté

$\frac{1}{2}$ oz. sea palm
1$\frac{1}{2}$ cups water, for soaking
1 cup fresh water, for cooking
1 Tbsp. toasted sesame oil
2 cloves garlic (minced)
1 Tbsp. natural soy sauce
$\frac{1}{4}$ cup water

1. Rinse sea palm and soak in 1$\frac{1}{2}$ cups water for 15 minutes.
2. Drain sea palm and discard soaking water. Cut into 2-inch lengths.
3. Place sea palm in saucepan with 1 cup fresh water. Cover and simmer about 20 minutes.
4. Remove cover and simmer another 5 to 7 minutes, allowing any remaining liquid to cook off.
5. Heat oil in a skillet over medium-high flame. Sauté the garlic for 15 seconds.
6. Add the sea palm and sauté for 3 minutes, tossing to coat all pieces with the garlic and oil.
7. Reduce the flame to low. Add $\frac{1}{4}$ cup water and the soy sauce. Cover and simmer 10 minutes.

Servings: 4

Salads

Salads lighten a meal and refresh us. They cool the body and balance heavier meals. Salads also cleanse the palate of other tastes and help speed digestion. For these reasons, they often come at the end of a meal, especially in Europe where traditional ways of eating still linger.

Because salads are light and cooling, we tend to eat more of them in spring and summer. Winter is the time for heartier meals with more breads and sauces. Too many raw vegetables, especially in the winter, can make us weak, tired, and more susceptible to colds and flu.

Most of us think of salads as merely a mixture of greens and dressings. To awaken you to their many varieties, I offer an assortment of different salads, all designed to be quick and easy to prepare. And all thoroughly satisfying, no matter what the season.

Texas-Style Corn Bread Salad

Add a pinch of dried sage or poultry seasoning, if desired.

> 4 cups Special Corn Bread, page 107 (crumbled)
> 1 cup tofu mayonnaise
> 2 celery ribs (sliced)
> 1 bell pepper (chopped)
> 1 cup scallions (sliced)
> ¾ cup pecan pieces (lightly roasted)
> ¾ tsp. sea salt

1. Combine all ingredients in a mixing bowl. Mix well.
2. Chill at least 2 hours before serving.
Servings: 6 to 8

Wild Rice Cranberry Salad

> 1 onion (diced)
> 1 clove garlic (minced)
> 3 Tbsp. olive oil
> ½ tsp. sea salt
> 1½ cups wild rice
> 3 cups vegetable stock or water
> 1 cup cranberries
> 1 cup water
> ½ cup maple syrup
> 1 cup scallions (sliced)
> ½ cup slivered almonds (roasted)

1. In a heavy 3-quart saucepan, sauté onion and garlic in olive oil for about 5 minutes.
2. Add salt, wild rice, and stock or water. Bring to a boil.
3. Lower flame. Cover and simmer approximately 50 minutes.
4. Boil cranberries for 5 minutes in water sweetened with maple syrup. Drain cranberries.
5. Add cranberries to rice. Stir in scallions and simmer 2 or 3 minutes.
6. Add almonds just before serving.

Servings: 6 to 8

Pasta with Tarragon Vinaigrette

> 10 oz. rotini pasta (cooked)
> 4 scallions (thinly sliced)
> ¼ cup parsley (chopped)
> 1 yellow squash (cut in matchsticks)
> 1 cucumber (seeded and cut in half-rounds)
> **Tarragon Vinaigrette**
> ½ cup extra-virgin olive oil

¼ **cup apple-cider vinegar**
1½ **tsp. dry mustard**
½ **tsp. dried oregano**
1 **tsp. dried basil**
¼ **tsp. dried tarragon**
1 **clove garlic (minced)**
½ **tsp. sea salt**

1. Combine all vinaigrette ingredients in a screw-top jar and shake well.
2. Pour vinaigrette over cooked pasta.
3. Add remaining ingredients and toss lightly.

Servings: 4 or 5

Soba Noodles with Pesto Dressing

Fresh spinach leaves may be substituted for basil.

3 cups fresh basil leaves
8 oz. soba noodles (cooked and drained)
Pesto Dressing
    1 Tbsp. olive oil
    2 Tbsp. almonds (chopped)
    2 Tbsp. mellow white miso
    2 cloves garlic (minced)

1. Chop basil and combine with hot soba in a large mixing bowl.
2. Blenderize dressing ingredients.
3. Toss dressing with pasta and basil.

Servings: 3

Oriental Udon Salad

>9 oz. udon noodles (cooked and drained)
>1 cup water chestnuts (sliced)
>2 cups mushrooms (sliced)
>1 bunch scallions (thinly sliced)
>3 Tbsp. fresh ginger root (grated)
>5 cloves garlic (minced)
>1/4 cup toasted sesame oil
>1/4 cup natural soy sauce
>1 tsp. maple syrup
>2 Tbsp. peanuts (chopped)
>8 to 10 lettuce leaves

1. Place cooked udon in a large mixing bowl with water chestnuts, mushrooms, and scallions.
2. Combine ginger, garlic, oil, soy sauce, and maple syrup. Toss with udon.
3. Cover and refrigerate for at least 1 hour. Add peanuts just before serving.
4. Serve each serving on a lettuce leaf.

Servings: 8 to 10

Wild Rice Salad

>2 cups water
>1/4 tsp. sea salt
>1 cup wild rice (washed and drained)
>kernels cut from 4 ears fresh corn
>1/2 cup scallions (thinly sliced)
>1 tsp. Dijon-style mustard
>1 tsp. maple syrup
>3 Tbsp. umeboshi vinegar
>3 Tbsp. extra-virgin olive oil

1. Bring water to a boil in heavy saucepan. Add salt and wild rice.
2. Cover pan and lower flame. Simmer gently 45 minutes.
3. Turn flame off but leave pan covered 10 minutes.
4. Transfer rice to a mixing bowl. Stir in the corn and scallions.
5. Using a whisk, blend together the mustard, syrup, vinegar, and oil, in another bowl.
6. Pour over the rice and mix gently before serving.

Servings: 6

Tabouli Salad

There are many different tabouli salads but this one is really good. The secret is using just the right amount of water.

1 tsp. sea salt
1½ cups boiling water
2 cups bulgur
½ cup olive oil
4 Tbsp. lemon juice (freshly squeezed)
2 cloves garlic (minced)
6 scallions (thinly sliced)
1 Tbsp. dried mint
½ cup parsley (chopped)

1. Dissolve salt in boiling water and pour over bulgur in a mixing bowl. Cover for 30 minutes.
2. Combine oil and lemon juice. Add to bulgur.
3. Stir in the garlic, scallions, mint, and parsley.
4. Marinate the salad in the refrigerator for 4 to 12 hours before serving. A minimum of 4 hours is needed to allow the flavors to mingle and to soften the bulgur.

Servings: 6 to 8

Wheat Berry Salad

Wheat berries may be cooked in a heavy saucepan if a pressure cooker is not available. Increase cooking time to one hour; increase water to three cups.

> 1 cup wheat berries (washed and drained)
> water
> 1/4 tsp. sea salt
> 2 Tbsp. lemon juice
> 2 Tbsp. extra-virgin olive oil
> 1 green bell pepper (seeded and minced)

1. Soak wheat berries overnight in 2 cups water. Drain and reserve soaking water. Add enough additional water to the soaking water to make a total of 1 1/2 cups.
2. Place water, salt, and soaked wheat berries in a pressure cooker. Fasten down the cover and bring to pressure. Lower flame and simmer 45 minutes.
3. Turn flame off and allow pressure to return to normal. Drain wheat berries and discard excess cooking liquid.
4. Transfer wheat berries to a mixing bowl and allow them to cool.
5. Fold in lemon juice, oil, and bell pepper.

Servings: 4

Quinoa Salad

> 3 3/4 cups water
> 1/2 tsp. sea salt
> 2 cups quinoa (washed and drained)
> 1/4 cup lemon juice (freshly squeezed)
> 1/4 cup sesame oil
> 2 Tbsp. toasted sesame oil
> 1 cup cucumber (seeded and chopped)

1 cup scallions (thinly sliced)
½ cup parsley (chopped)
¼ cup sesame seeds (lightly roasted)

1. Bring water to a boil in a heavy saucepan.
2. Add salt and quinoa. Lower flame. Cover and simmer 20 minutes.
3. Turn flame off and let sit 5 minutes before removing lid.
4. Stir in the lemon juice and oils. Add cucumber, scallions, and parsley. Mix thoroughly.
5. Just before serving, sprinkle with the sesame seeds.

Servings: 6 to 8

Rotini Pasta Salad

I like to use spelt rotini for this dish. It holds its shape well and is a nice change from wheat pasta. If desired, the snow peas can be dipped in boiling water for ten seconds before adding to the salad to bring out their deep green color.

10 oz. rotini pasta (cooked)
1 cup carrots (cut in thin matchsticks)
1 tsp. sesame seeds (roasted)
¼ cup natural soy sauce
1 Tbsp. ginger juice (squeezed from grated fresh ginger root)
3 Tbsp. toasted sesame oil
3 Tbsp. lemon juice (freshly squeezed)
6 scallions (thinly sliced)
1 Tbsp. garlic (minced)
1 cup snow peas

1. Combine all ingredients in a large mixing bowl.
2. Cover and place in refrigerator for 30 minutes before serving.

Servings: 4 or 5

Millet "Potato" Salad

Does this taste a lot like potato salad? You'll never miss potato salad once you've tried this dish. "Potato" salad better than you ever dreamed and without the nightshades.

> 3³/₄ cups water
> ¹/₂ tsp. sea salt
> 1 cup millet
> 1 red onion (finely minced)
> 2 ribs celery (finely minced)
> ¹/₂ cup sweet pickle relish
> 4 Tbsp. tofu mayonnaise
> ¹/₄ tsp. celery seed, optional
> ¹/₂ tsp. dried dillweed

1. Bring 3¹/₂ cups salted water to a boil. Add millet.
2. Cover and lower flame. Simmer 40 minutes.
3. Transfer cooked millet to a 9-inch-square dish. Press millet to make compact. Allow to cool about 30 to 45 minutes.
4. When cool, cut millet into small cubes and place in mixing bowl.
5. Add remaining ingredients and mix gently.

Servings: 4 to 5

Soba Noodle Avocado Salad with Lemon Sesame Dressing

Lemon sesame dressing really makes it wonderful. Try a garnish of toasted and crushed dulse seaweed.

> 9 oz. soba noodles (cooked)
> 2 avocados (sliced)
> 1 cucumber (seeded and sliced)
> 4 scallions (thinly sliced)

Lemon Sesame Dressing
>   **4 Tbsp. natural soy sauce**
>   **4 Tbsp. lemon juice (freshly squeezed)**
>   **2 tsp. toasted sesame oil**

1. Mound soba noodles in a large bowl. Decorate with avocado slices, cucumber, and scallions.
2. Combine dressing ingredients and pour over the noodles.

Servings: 4 or 5

Udon Salad with Sesame Ginger Sauce

>   **1 cup snow peas (strings removed)**
>   **1 carrot (cut in matchsticks)**
>   **9 oz. udon noodles (cooked)**
>   **3 Tbsp. sesame seeds (roasted)**

Sesame Ginger Sauce
>   **4 Tbsp. sesame oil**
>   **2 Tbsp. natural soy sauce**
>   **2 Tbsp. brown-rice vinegar**
>   **2 tsp. toasted sesame oil**
>   **$1\frac{1}{2}$ tsp. ginger juice (squeezed from grated fresh ginger root)**
>   **1 tsp. maple syrup**

1. Blanch vegetables in boiling water. Rinse in cold water and drain.
2. Whisk sauce ingredients in small mixing bowl.
3. Place noodles, vegetables, and sesame seeds in a large bowl and combine with sauce.

Servings: 4 or 5

Crispy Napa Salad

I serve this salad garnished with pickled red cabbage, cucumbers, and snow peas.

> **4 cups napa cabbage (cut in thin matchsticks)**
> **3 romaine lettuce leaves (cut in thin matchsticks)**
> **5 Tbsp. Mustard Vinaigrette Dressing, page 161**

1. Mix and toss with dressing.

Servings: 8 to 10

Pea Pod Salad with Sesame Dressing

> **4 cups napa cabbage (cut in matchsticks)**
> **1 cup pea pods (cut diagonally)**
> **1/2 cup mushrooms (quartered)**
> **1 carrot (cut in matchsticks)**
> **2 scallions (thinly sliced)**
> **2 Tbsp. sesame seeds (roasted)**
>
> **Sesame Dressing**
> **1/4 cup rice vinegar**
> **1/4 cup safflower oil**
> **1 Tbsp. natural soy sauce**
> **1 tsp. maple syrup**
> **1/4 tsp. toasted sesame oil**

1. Combine cabbage, pea pods, mushrooms, carrots, and scallions in a mixing bowl.
2. Combine dressing ingredients in a screw-top jar. Cover and shake to mix.
3. Pour dressing over salad. Toss gently to mix.
4. Sprinkle with sesame seeds and toss again.

Servings: 8 to 10

Oriental Cucumber Salad

1½ cucumbers (peeled, seeded, and sliced)
1 tsp. sea salt
2 Tbsp. rice vinegar
2 Tbsp. toasted sesame oil
1 Tbsp. natural soy sauce
2 tsp. maple syrup or barley malt
2 tsp. ginger juice (squeezed from grated fresh ginger root)

1. Place cucumbers in a mixing bowl. Combine with salt and chill 1 hour.
2. Drain cucumbers.
3. Combine remaining ingredients and pour over cucumbers. Toss to coat.

Servings: 4 to 6

Quick Coleslaw

¾ cup tofu mayonnaise
2 Tbsp. Dijon-style mustard
3 Tbsp. liquid from jar of natural dill pickles
⅔ cup scallions (sliced)
8 cups cabbage (shredded)
½ tsp. sea salt or to taste

1. Combine first 4 ingredients in a small mixing bowl.
2. Place cabbage in a large mixing bowl. Add mayonnaise mixture and toss until thoroughly mixed.
3. Add salt to taste.
4. Cover and refrigerate for several hours before serving.

Servings: 12 to 14

Carrot Salad

1 Tbsp. natural soy sauce
1 Tbsp. rice vinegar
4 carrots (cut in thin matchsticks)
½ cup raisins (soaked in hot water and drained)
½ onion (sliced in thin rings)
5 or 6 lettuce leaves

1. Make a dressing by combining soy sauce and rice vinegar.
2. Combine carrots, raisins, and onion in a bowl.
3. Add the dressing and toss.
4. Serve each serving on a lettuce leaf.
Servings: 5 or 6

Waldorf Salad

This is a twist on a great salad that I learned from my grandmother. Prepare it at least two hours in advance to allow flavors
to blend.

2 apples (unpeeled and cubed)
juice of 2 oranges
16 oz. firm-style tofu (finely diced)
lightly salted water to cover
2 carrots (finely diced and blanched)
1 cup walnut pieces
1 stalk celery (sliced)
1 cup raisins (soaked and drained)
½ tsp. dried tarragon
¼ tsp. sea salt
2 Tbsp. tofu mayonnaise

1. Combine apples and orange juice in mixing bowl.
2. Simmer tofu in lightly salted water to cover for 3 minutes.
   Drain well.

3. Combine all ingredients. Chill at least 2 hours before serving.
Servings: 14 to 16

Carrot Raisin Salad

> **3 cups carrots (grated)**
> **½ cup raisins**
> **Dressing**
> **6 Tbsp. olive oil**
> **2 Tbsp. lemon juice (freshly squeezed)**
> **2 tsp. barley malt, rice syrup, or maple syrup**
> **1 tsp. prepared mustard**

1. Combine carrots and raisins in a mixing bowl.
2. In a separate bowl, whisk the dressing ingredients until creamy.
3. Toss the dressing with the carrots and raisins.
Servings: 4 to 6

Carrot and Apple Slaw

> **2 Tbsp. lemon juice (freshly squeezed)**
> **1 Tbsp. natural apple jelly**
> **4 carrots (peeled and grated)**
> **1 golden delicious apple (peeled and grated)**
> **⅓ cup roasted cashews (chopped)**
> **⅓ cup raisins**
> **¼ tsp. sea salt or to taste**

1. In a large bowl whisk lemon juice and jelly to blend.
2. Add carrots, apples, cashews, and raisins. Toss.
3. Season to taste with salt.
Servings: 8

Humus

During summer, try serving a three-salad platter of one large scoop each of Humus, Tabouli, and Millet "Potato" Salad on a bed of lettuce with a freshly made breadstick. Humus also can be used as a dip with chips or Quick Boiled Vegetables.

2 cups cooked chickpeas
3 Tbsp. raw sesame tahini
2 cloves garlic (minced)
3 Tbsp. natural soy sauce
3 Tbsp. lemon juice (freshly squeezed)

1. Combine all ingredients in a blender or food processor. If necessary, add 1 or 2 tablespoons chickpea cooking liquid or water for easier blending.
2. Process until smooth.

Servings: 8 to 10

Gingered Humus

Use as a spread on rice cakes or as a dip with lightly steamed vegetable sticks.

2 cups cooked chickpeas
2 cloves garlic (minced)
3 Tbsp. lemon juice (freshly squeezed)
3 Tbsp. raw sesame tahini
3 Tbsp. natural soy sauce
1 Tbsp. ginger juice (squeezed from grated fresh ginger
  root)
1 Tbsp. toasted sesame oil

1. Place chickpeas in food processor with minced garlic.
2. Process at high speed until mixture is smooth. If mixture is too thick, add 2 tablespoons chickpea cooking liquid or water.

3. Add remaining ingredients and process until smooth. Taste and adjust seasoning.

Servings: 8 to 10

Garbanzo and Green Bean Salad

2 cups water
3 cups fresh green beans (tips removed
and cut in 3-inch lengths)
2 cups cooked chickpeas
1 cup celery (thinly sliced)
1 clove garlic (minced)
¼ cup apple-cider vinegar
¼ cup canola oil
1 Tbsp. maple syrup
½ tsp. sea salt
½ tsp. dried basil

1. Bring water to a boil. Add green beans and cover. Simmer approximately 5 minutes or until just tender. Drain.
2. In a mixing bowl, combine green beans, chickpeas, celery, and garlic.
3. In a separate bowl, combine remaining ingredients. Blend well and pour over bean mixture.
4. Toss gently until well coated.
5. Cover and refrigerate for several hours before serving.

Servings: 8 to 10

Pinto Bean Salad

Try serving this salad on a lettuce leaf to accompany brown rice and steamed vegetables.

> **4 cups cooked pinto beans**
> **2 tsp. garlic (minced)**
> **½ cup parsley (coarsely chopped)**
> **3 Tbsp. extra-virgin olive oil**
> **1 tsp. sea salt**

1. Drain beans
2. In a large mixing bowl, combine all ingredients.
Servings: 8

Pressed Salad

Pressed vegetables retain vitamins, minerals, and enzymes. Serve with brown rice for a very good combination.

> **1 cup green cabbage (thinly sliced)**
> **¼ cup celery (thinly sliced)**
> **½ cup onion (sliced in thin half-rounds)**
> **¼ cup cucumber (seeded and sliced)**
> **½ tsp. sea salt**
> **1 tsp. brown-rice vinegar**

1. Place first 4 ingredients in a mixing bowl.
2. Thoroughly mix salt and vinegar with vegetables.
3. Transfer ingredients to a pickle press. Tighten the lid and apply pressure. Let sit for 1 or 2 hours before removing cover.
4. Place vegetables in a serving bowl. If vegetables are too salty, quickly rinse under cold water and squeeze out liquid before serving.
Servings: 4 to 6

Simple Pressed Salad

2 cups Chinese cabbage (very thinly shredded)
¼ cup celery (thinly sliced on diagonal)
½ cup red radishes (thinly sliced)
1 tsp. sea salt

1. Place all vegetables in a pickle press. Add the salt and mix well.
2. Place the top on the press and apply pressure.
3. Let sit for 1½ to 2 hours.
4. Remove vegetables from the press and squeeze out all the liquid.
5. Mix vegetables together in a serving dish.

Servings: 5 or 6

Rutabaga Pickles

2 rutabagas (thinly sliced)
½ cup natural soy sauce
½ cup water

1. Place rutabagas in a salad press.
2. Combine soy sauce and water. Pour over rutabagas.
3. Apply pressure by placing the top on the salad press.
4. Allow to pickle overnight.

Yield: 3 cups

Daikon Ume Pickles

Great served as a condiment with whole grains.

1 cup daikon (cut in matchsticks)
2 Tbsp. umeboshi vinegar

1. Place daikon in a flat dish. Sprinkle vinegar over daikon.
2. Let marinate for 1 hour, stirring occasionally.
Yield: 1 cup

Quick Daikon Pickles

1 cup daikon (cut in thin half-rounds)
$\frac{1}{2}$ cup natural soy sauce
5 Tbsp. water
$\frac{1}{4}$ cup lemon juice (freshly squeezed)

1. Place daikon in a jar.
2. Mix soy sauce, water, and lemon juice.
3. Pour over daikon, making sure that all pieces are covered. Let marinate overnight.
Yield: 1 cup

Quick Onion Pickles

Be sure to purchase natural dill pickles.

2 onions, red or white
1 cup dill-pickle juice

1. Slice the onions in crescents and place in a clean jar.
2. Pour the pickle juice over the onions.
3. Let marinate 1 or 2 hours.
Yield: 2 to 3 cups

Quick Breads

Baking says love. The aroma from fresh bread, muffins, and cakes fills your kitchen and draws people together. There's something magical and even nostalgic about baked foods. They remind us of childhood and the best parts of ourselves. They raise the spirit and warm the heart. They say someone cares.

Baked foods are satisfying as no other food can be. They have texture, crunch, and weight. They are nutritious, essential, and just plain good. They can be picked up in our hands and eaten, bringing us in touch with our most basic, primitive, and unpretentious selves. No other food is more wholesome and universal. It is food for the spirit as well as the body.

Baking is one of the most creative things you can do. It's also one of the most satisfying. When you draw from your oven a rich loaf of bread or a beautiful pan of muffins, you feel you've created something special.

Baking concentrates the power of the grain. In macrobiotic parlance, it makes it more yang and contracted. Therefore, like most people, I do more baking in the fall and winter, when nature itself is contracting, forcing its own life force down into the earth and roots of the trees. Spring is when energy rises from the depths of the earth, into the trunks and branches of the trees. Summer expands the energy to the peripheri of the trees, their leaves and fruits. Baking coincides with fall and winter energy. Most of us know this intuitively and therefore spend more time in the kitchen during winter, when we like to bake all kinds of goodies.

After fifteen years of study and observation, I have learned that people recognize that each grain product has its own unique taste and effect. Corn bread, for example, is a happy food. It's an invitation to sit down and enjoy yourself. Wheat, on the other hand, is serious nutrition and taste. I recommend that you try all the recipes in this chapter and see for yourself the different effect each has on you and your friends and loved ones.

Tofu Carrot Corn Bread

16 oz. firm-style tofu
1 cup vegetable stock or water
½ cup corn oil
2 cups cornmeal
1 tsp. aluminum-free baking powder
1 tsp. sea salt
1 tsp. dried marjoram, dried basil, or other dried herb
3 carrots (grated)
1 onion (finely diced)
1 cup fresh corn (kernels cut from cob)

1. Preheat oven to 375 degrees. Oil a 9-inch-square baking dish.
2. Blend tofu, stock, and oil in a food processor until smooth.
3. Combine cornmeal, baking powder, salt, and marjoram in a large mixing bowl.
4. Stir wet mixture into dry ingredients. Fold in carrots, onion, and corn.
5. Pour into the oiled baking dish. Bake at 375 degrees for 45 minutes.

Servings: 9

Old-Fashioned Corn Bread

 ¾ cup corn oil
 ¼ cup maple syrup
 4 oz. tofu
 2 cups water
 2 cups cornmeal
 1 Tbsp. aluminum-free baking powder
 ½ tsp. sea salt

1. Preheat oven to 375 degrees. Oil a 9-inch cast-iron skillet.
2. Combine first 4 ingredients in a blender. Blend until creamy.
3. Combine remaining ingredients in a separate bowl.
4. Stir the wet ingredients into the dry ingredients.
5. Pour batter into the skillet. Bake 20 minutes at 375 degrees.
Servings: 8

Special Corn Bread

 2 cups cornmeal
 1 cup whole-wheat pastry flour
 1 Tbsp. aluminum-free baking powder
 1 tsp. sea salt
 3 Tbsp. tofu mayonnaise
 2 cups water

1. Preheat oven to 375 degrees. Oil a 9-inch cast-iron skillet.
2. Combine first 4 ingredients in a mixing bowl.
3. Purée mayonnaise and water in a food processor or blender until smooth.
4. Stir the wet ingredients into the dry ingredients and mix well.
5. Pour batter into the skillet and bake 25 minutes at 375 degrees.
Servings: 8

Corn Bread

> 1 cup cornmeal
> 1 cup whole-wheat pastry flour
> 1 Tbsp. aluminum-free baking powder
> pinch sea salt
> 1 cup soy milk
> 1/4 cup corn oil
> 4 Tbsp. maple syrup

1. Preheat oven to 350 degrees. Oil a 8- or 9-inch baking pan.
2. Combine first 4 ingredients in a mixing bowl.
3. Combine remaining ingredients in a separate bowl, using a wire whisk to blend until smooth.
4. Add wet ingredients to dry ingredients and combine.
5. Pour into the oiled baking pan. Bake at 350 degrees for approximately 50 minutes.

Servings: 8

Spelt Corn Bread

> 1 cup cornmeal
> 1 cup spelt flour
> 2 tsp. aluminum-free baking powder
> 1/2 tsp. sea salt
> 2 tsp. maple syrup
> 1 1/2 cups soy milk, rice milk, or water
> 3 Tbsp. tofu mayonnaise

1. Preheat oven to 425 degrees. Oil a 8- or 9-inch baking pan.
2. Combine first 4 ingredients in a mixing bowl.
3. Dissolve the maple syrup into the soy milk and add the mayonnaise.
4. Stir the wet ingredients into the dry ingredients.

5. Pour batter into the oiled baking pan. Bake at 425 degrees for 20 to 25 minutes.

Servings: 8

Sweet Corn Bread

> 1 cup cornmeal
> 1/2 cup whole-wheat pastry flour
> 1/2 cup unbleached flour
> 2 tsp. aluminum-free baking powder
> 1/2 tsp. baking soda
> 1/8 tsp. sea salt
> 1 cup water
> 4 Tbsp. corn oil
> 3 Tbsp. maple syrup
> 2 tsp. rice vinegar

1. Preheat oven to 400 degrees.
2. Mix the liquid ingredients and dry ingredients separately.
3. Add liquid ingredients to dry ingredients and combine.
4. Pour into an oiled 8- or 9-inch cast-iron skillet. Bake at 400 degrees for 25 to 30 minutes.

Servings: 8

Sweet Corn Muffins

I like this with a bowl of pinto bean soup and a slice of red onion.

> **16 oz. firm-style tofu**
> **1 cup soy milk or apple juice**
> **¼ cup water**
> **3 Tbsp. maple syrup**
> **3 Tbsp. corn oil**
> **1¼ cups whole-wheat pastry flour**
> **3½ tsp. aluminum-free baking powder**
> **1 tsp. sea salt**
> **¼ cup cornmeal**
> **1 cup fresh corn (kernels cut from cob)**

1. Preheat oven to 400 degrees. Oil muffin pans well.
2. Blend first 5 ingredients until creamy, in a blender or food
   processor.
3. Combine flour, baking powder, salt, and cornmeal in a mixing bowl.
4. Stir wet ingredients into dry ingredients and combine well.
5. Stir in corn.
6. Fill well-oiled muffin pans two-thirds full. Bake at 400 degrees 25 to 30 minutes.

Yield: 12 muffins

Cranberry Corn Muffins

> **¾ cup cornmeal**
> **¼ cup oat flakes**
> **1 cup whole-wheat pastry flour**
> **1 Tbsp. aluminum-free baking powder**
> **½ tsp. sea salt**
> **1 cup apple juice**

8 oz. firm-style tofu
3½ Tbsp. corn oil
5 Tbsp. maple syrup
½ cup cranberries

1. Preheat oven to 375 degrees. Oil muffin pans.
2. Combine the first 5 ingredients in a mixing bowl.
3. Combine apple juice, tofu, oil, and syrup in blender or food processor. Blend until creamy smooth.
4. Add liquid ingredients to dry ingredients and mix gently.
5. Stir in cranberries.
6. Fill oiled muffin pans and bake 20 minutes at 375 degrees.

Yield: 8 muffins

Texas Corn Fritters

This is a tasty "bread" that can be served with soup.

1¼ cups whole-wheat pastry flour
⅛ tsp. granulated garlic
⅓ tsp. granulated onion
⅓ tsp. turmeric
1 Tbsp. dried basil
1 tsp. sea salt
2½ tsp. aluminum-free baking powder
1 cup soy milk
⅔ cup fresh corn (kernels cut from cob)
2 Tbsp. corn oil

1. Combine first 7 ingredients in a large mixing bowl.
2. Stir in soy milk to make batter. Fold in corn kernels.
3. Preheat a skillet over medium-high heat. Add 2 tablespoons corn oil.
4. Drop fritters into hot skillet, using a tablespoon.
5. Brown fritters on both sides, adding a bit more oil if needed.

Yield: 8 to 10 fritters

Quick Corn Cakes

Try these hot out of the oven and spread with Millet "Butter."
Great with any meal.

>1 cup cornmeal
>4 Tbsp. soy flour
>$\frac{1}{2}$ tsp. sea salt
>1 cup boiling water
>2 cups cooked short-grain brown rice
>$\frac{1}{2}$ cup sunflower seeds (ground)

1. Preheat oven to 400 degrees. Oil a cookie sheet.
2. Combine first 3 ingredients in a mixing bowl.
3. Add boiling water and mix well. Stir in rice and seeds.
4. Using an ice-cream scoop, place scoops of dough 1 inch apart on the oiled cookie sheet. Flatten slightly into cakes.
5. Bake at 400 degrees for 30 minutes.

Yield: 10 to 12 corn cakes

Southern Corn Bread Dressing

>1 pan baked Special Corn Bread, page 107
>2 to 3 cups boiling water
>4 slices whole-wheat bread
>5 ribs celery (minced)
>1 medium onion (minced)
>$\frac{1}{2}$ tsp. dried sage
>$\frac{1}{2}$ tsp. poultry seasoning
>$\frac{1}{2}$ tsp. salt

1. Preheat oven to 400 degrees. Oil a 9x12-inch baking pan.
2. Crumble corn bread into mixing bowl. Pour enough boiling water over corn bread to make a slightly wet, pourable mixture. Set aside while preparing the remaining ingredients.
3. Tear whole-wheat bread into pieces and add to corn-bread

mixture.

4. Add remaining ingredients and mix well.

5. Transfer to the oiled baking pan. Bake at 400 degrees approximately 45 to 50 minutes or until firm.

Servings: 12

Unyeasted Bread Sticks

Terrific with a bowl of soup. Also, good travel food.

> **3 cups whole-wheat flour**
> **1¾ cup oat flour**
> **1⅔ cup water**
> **2 tsp. sea salt**
> **1½ Tbsp. maple syrup**
> **⅓ cup shredded coconut**
> **¾ cup sunflower seeds**

1. Preheat oven to 325 degrees. Lightly oil a large cookie sheet.

2. Combine wheat and oat flour in a large mixing bowl.

3. Blend remaining ingredients in a blender or food processor until smooth.

4. Combine wet and dry ingredients.

5. Pinch off a bit of dough and roll between your hands to form a stick about the size of a pencil. Place on the oiled cookie sheet. Repeat until all dough is used. Use unbleached flour to keep your hands from getting sticky.

6. Bake for 18 minutes at 325 degrees.

7. Turn sticks over and bake 8 minutes longer.

8. Cool completely before storing. Bread sticks keep about a week in the refrigerator.

Yield: 36 bread sticks

Entreés

An entrée is something out of the ordinary — something that has a little more flair, pizzaz, and dazzle. It's exciting to make an entrée and present it to your family or guests. It's a statement: You took a little more time; you went to a little greater effort. You're marking the occasion with a meal that is artistic and wonderful.

For all of these reasons, entrées are great for celebrations or special occasions. Many of the entrées I present here look and taste like the meat loaves, hamburgers, or croquettes that many Americans eat every day. There are some differences in taste — I believe that my entrées are a lot better tasting than your average meat loaf or hamburger helper — and there's a big difference in the health effects of these dishes. The entrées described here will support your health, not weaken it, as the standard American meal will.

Entrées often take a little more time and care in the preparation but they're worth it. However, there are ways to shorten the time and present a quick entrée that looks and tastes like you've been in the kitchen all day. The way to do it is to use leftover grains and combine them in a variety of ways, and then add a nice sauce. For example, you can take leftover millet, tofu, vegetables, and herbs, and combine them for a delicious millet croquette. Add one of the wonderful gravies I present in Sauces and Dressings, pages 144-170, and you've got something really special. The fact is, these croquettes take very little effort and even less time to prepare.

In a few minutes, you can turn leftover grains and beans into a variety of loaves, burgers, and croquettes. Add the sauce and . . . Well, give it a try, and you'll see the results in your family's smiling eyes.

Rice Walnut Loaf

This is a good dish to serve for company or at holiday time. It can be made one day ahead and reheated. Slice and serve with Very Good Brown Sauce or with a gravy or sauce of your choice.

> ¾ cup water
> ⅓ cup natural soy sauce
> 2 cloves garlic (minced)
> ½ tsp. dried sage
> ¼ tsp. dried basil
> ½ tsp. celery salt
> ¼ cup sunflower seeds (ground)
> 2 tsp. sesame oil
> 4 cups cooked short-grain brown rice
> 5 cups soft whole-wheat bread crumbs
> 1 cup celery (minced)
> 2 cups onions (minced)
> 1¾ cups walnuts (ground)

1. Preheat oven to 350 degrees. Oil a 9x12-inch baking dish.
2. Blenderize the first 8 ingredients.
3. Place rice in a large mixing bowl. Pour blended mixture over the rice and mix well.
4. Add bread crumbs to rice mixture. Stir in celery, onions, and walnuts.
5. Transfer to the oiled baking dish.
6. Cover and bake at 350 degrees for 35 minutes.
7. Remove cover and bake 10 minutes longer to brown.

Servings: 12

Savory Rice Loaf

2 cups onions (chopped and sautéed)
2½ cups cooked brown rice
½ cup celery (minced)
1 cup cashews (chopped)
1 cup vegetable broth or water
2 Tbsp. natural soy sauce
1 tsp. sea salt
1 Tbsp. granulated onion
1 Tbsp. granulated garlic
½ tsp. dried sage
½ tsp. dried thyme
2 cups whole-wheat bread crumbs

1. Preheat oven to 350 degrees. Oil a 9x12-inch baking dish.
2. Combine all ingredients. Place in the oiled baking dish.
3. Cover and bake 45 minutes at 350 degrees.
4. Uncover and bake 10 minutes longer or until firm.
Servings: 12

Easy Millet Squash Pie with Rich Carrot Sauce

7½ cups water
½ tsp. sea salt
3 to 4 cups butternut squash (cubed)
2 cups millet (washed and drained)
Rich Carrot Sauce
2 cups well-cooked carrots
1 Tbsp. raw sesame tahini
1 Tbsp. mellow white miso

1. Bring water to a boil in a heavy pot. Add salt, squash, and millet.

2. Reduce flame and place a heat diffuser under pot. Cover and simmer 45 minutes.
3. Turn flame off and leave pot covered 5 minutes.
4. Stir with a wooden spoon. Pour millet mixture into a pie plate and let cool until set.
5. Purée carrots, tahini, and miso in a blender to make a sauce.
6. Cut millet in wedges. Serve sauce over millet wedges.
Servings: 6

Millet with Mock Cheese Sauce

My friend, Ramona, thinks this is marvelous. You will too.

8 cups water
2 cups millet (washed and drained)
1/4 cup natural soy sauce
2 cloves garlic (minced)
1 carrot (cubed)
1 onion (minced)
Mock Cheese Sauce
   10 oz. firm-style tofu
   2 Tbsp. raw sesame tahini
   2 Tbsp. lemon juice (freshly squeezed)
   2 Tbsp. mellow white miso

1. Bring water to a boil. Add millet, soy sauce, garlic, carrot, and onion. Cover and simmer over low flame 45 minutes.
2. Spoon into a 9x12-inch baking dish, pressing to make a smooth surface. Let cool briefly while making sauce.
3. Preheat oven to 400 degrees.
4. Place sauce ingredients in blender and blend until smooth, adding a few tablespoons water, if needed.
5. Spread sauce over millet.
6. Bake at 400 degrees for 5 to 7 minutes, or until browned.
Servings: 10 to 12

Millet "Meatballs"

"Meatballs" like you've never tasted. Serve as an entrée or with udon noodles and Brown Gravy.

3½ cups water
¼ cup natural soy sauce
1 onion (minced)
1 carrot (grated)
1 cup millet (washed and drained)
1 cup walnuts (ground to fine meal)
⅓ cup whole-wheat flour
½ cup whole-wheat bread crumbs
2 tsp. granulated onion
2 tsp. granulated garlic
1 pinch dried sage
1 pinch dried basil

1. Bring water and soy sauce to a boil. Add onion, carrot, and millet.
2. Lower flame and place a heat diffuser under the pot. Cover and simmer 45 minutes.
3. Turn flame off and leave lid on for another 10 minutes. Then transfer millet to a large mixing bowl to cool, about 25 to 30 minutes.
4. Preheat oven to 300 degrees. Oil a cookie sheet.
5. Combine remaining ingredients and work this into the millet mixture with your hands.
6. Form into walnut-sized "meatballs" and place on the oiled cookie sheet.
7. Bake at 300 degrees for 40 minutes.

Yield: 12 to 16 "meatballs"

Millet and Kale with Tofu Spread

4 cups water
2 Tbsp. natural soy sauce
1 carrot (cut in matchsticks)
1 onion (minced)
2 cups cauliflower (coarsely chopped)
$\frac{1}{2}$ tsp. dried rosemary
1 pinch dried sage
1 pinch dried tarragon
$\frac{1}{4}$ tsp. sea salt
1 cup millet (washed and drained)
$\frac{1}{2}$ bunch kale or other greens (steamed)

Tofu Spread
10 oz. firm-style tofu
2 Tbsp. raw sesame tahini
2 Tbsp. lemon juice (freshly squeezed)
2 Tbsp. white miso

1. Bring water and soy sauce to a boil.
2. Add carrots, onion, cauliflower, herbs, and salt. When water boils again, stir in millet.
3. Lower flame and slip a heat diffuser under pot. Cover and simmer 45 minutes.
4. Transfer millet mixture to a 9-inch-square baking dish. Press millet down and let cool while preparing the tofu spread.
5. Preheat oven to 400 degrees.
6. Place tofu-spread ingredients in a blender and blend until creamy. Add a few tablespoons water if needed to blend.
7. Place a layer of kale over the millet in the baking dish. Drizzle the tofu spread over the kale.
8. Bake at 400 degrees until top turns brown, about 15 to 20 minutes.
9. Cut into squares to serve.

Servings: 6

Country Corn Bread Casserole

4 cups onions (coarsely chopped)
2 Tbsp. sesame oil
6 Tbsp. water
2 cups carrots (cut in chunks)
2 cups rutabagas (peeled and cut in chunks)
1 cup sunflower seeds (ground in blender)
½ cup cooked brown rice
½ tsp. sea salt
Special Corn Bread batter, page 107

1. Sauté onions in oil about 5 minutes.
2. Cover pot and cook over low flame about 15 minutes, or until liquid is released.
3. Add water, carrots, and rutabagas. Cover pot and simmer 15 to 20 minutes or until vegetables are tender, adding a little more water if needed.
4. Season with salt. Stir in the seeds and rice.
5. Transfer mixture to an oiled 9x12-inch baking pan.
6. Preheat oven to 400 degrees.
7. Make corn bread batter and pour an even layer of batter over the vegetable mixture.
8. Bake at 400 degrees 25 to 30 minutes or until corn bread is browned

Servings: 12

Mexican Chalupas

This is a popular entrée and is easy to prepare.

>1 scoop Texas-Style Polenta, page 36
>1 Tbsp. Refried Beans, page 79
>1 Tbsp. Bulgur Helper, page 34, optional
>1 dollop Tofu "Sour Cream," page 152
>1 Tbsp. lettuce (shredded)
>1 tsp. carrots (shredded)
>1 tsp. olives (sliced)
>blue corn chips for garnish

1. Place polenta on a plate. Ladle refried beans on top.
2. Sprinkle bulgur helper, if desired, over beans. Add a dollop of tofu "sour cream."
3. Garnish with lettuce, carrots, and olives.
4. Artfully arrange blue corn chips around the chalupa.

Servings: 1

Sweet and Sour Seitan

Great served over noodles.

>2 cups Sweet and Sour Sauce, page 151
>16 oz. seitan (thinly sliced)

1. Add thin slices of seitan to sauce and heat through (about 5 minutes).

Servings: 6 to 8

Udon with Peanut Dressing

> 7 oz. udon noodles (cooked and drained)
> 2 scallions (sliced)
>
> **Peanut Dressing**
> > 2 Tbsp. smooth peanut butter
> > 2 Tbsp. natural soy sauce
> > 2 to 4 Tbsp. water
> > 2 tsp. rice vinegar
> > 2 tsp. maple syrup
> > 1/8 tsp. dry ginger
> > 1/8 tsp. granulated garlic

1. Place cooked noodles in a bowl and keep warm.
2. Combine dressing ingredients in a small bowl and blend well.
3. Spoon sauce over noodles and garnish with sliced scallions.

Servings: 3 or 4

Azuki Beans with Udon Noodles

> 3/4 cup azuki beans (washed and drained)
> 1 strip kombu , 2 inches long and 1 inch wide
> 3 1/2 cups water
> 1/4 tsp. sea salt
> 1 tsp. natural soy sauce
> 1 lb. udon noodles (cooked)
> 3 scallions (thinly sliced)

1. Place azuki beans, kombu, and water in a saucepan. Cover and bring to a boil over high flame.
2. Lower flame. Cover and simmer until soft, about 1 hour.
3. Add salt and soy sauce. Simmer 15 minutes longer.
4. Transfer azuki beans to a large mixing bowl.

5. Combine udon noodles with azuki beans and mix gently.
6. Place in a 9x12-inch casserole dish and let stand 10 minutes.
7. Cut in squares to serve. Garnish with scallions.
Servings: 12

Spelt Pasta with Chickpea Sauce

> **2 quarts water**
> **2 cups spelt rotini**
> Chickpea Sauce
> > **1 cup Chickpeas with Kombu, page 73**
> > **$\frac{1}{2}$ cup parsley (chopped)**
> > **1 small carrot (quartered)**
> > **2 Tbsp. sesame tahini**
> > **$\frac{1}{4}$ cup onion (finely diced)**
> > **2 Tbsp. umeboshi vinegar**
> > **$\frac{1}{2}$ cup water**

1. Bring 2 quarts water to a boil and add rotini.
2. Cook according to directions on package. Rinse and drain.
3. Place rotini in a large bowl and set aside.
4. Place the sauce ingredients in a blender. Blend until smooth.
5. Place pasta in individual serving dishes. Spoon 4 or 5 table-spoons of sauce over each serving of pasta.
Servings: 4

Chickpea Croquettes

3 cups cooked short-grain brown rice
1½ cups cooked chickpeas (mashed)
1 tsp. sea salt
1 Tbsp. granulated onion
1 tsp. dried thyme
oil for deep-frying

1. Combine all ingredients except oil in a large mixing bowl.
2. Form into croquettes with wet hands.
3. To deep-fry, make sure oil is very hot, but not smoking. Gently lower one croquette into the hot oil. Deep-fry until brown on both sides. Do not add another croquette until the first one has been cooked and removed from the oil.
4. Drain on paper towels.

Yield: 12 croquettes

Lima Bean Cakes

Use frozen lima beans for a quick dish.

2 cups lima beans (cooked and mashed)
1 cup soft whole-wheat bread crumbs
½ cup cooked short-grain brown rice
½ cup onion (minced)
¾ tsp. dried sage
¾ tsp. sea salt

1. Combine all ingredients in a mixing bowl.
2. With wet hands, form into cakes about ½ inch thick.
3. Brown on both sides in an oiled skillet.

Yield: 6 to 8 cakes

Lentil Grain Loaf

Great sliced and served with gravy.

> **2 cups green lentils (washed and drained)**
> **6 cups water**
> **1 cup bulgur**
> **2 cups water**
> **1 cup soft whole-wheat bread crumbs**
> **1½ cups cooked brown rice**
> **1 onion (minced)**
> **1 clove garlic (minced)**
> **1 tsp. dried thyme**
> **1 tsp. dried oregano**
> **1 tsp. dried tarragon**
> **1 to 2 tsp. sea salt**

1. Cook lentils in 6 cups water for 40 minutes.
2. Cook bulgur in 2 cups water for 15 minutes.
3. Preheat oven to 350 degrees.
4. Drain cooked lentils if liquid remains. Combine with bulgur in a mixing bowl.
5. Add remaining ingredients and mix well.
6. Transfer mixture to an oiled pan and shape into a loaf.
7. Cover and bake 45 minutes at 350 degrees.

Servings: 10 to 12

Lentil Loaf

2 cups cooked lentils
1/2 cup cashews, blended with 1/2 cup water
1 cup cooked brown rice
2 cups whole-wheat bread crumbs
1 cup walnuts (ground)
1 tsp. sea salt
1/2 tsp. dried sage
1 cup carrots (grated)
1 cup celery (minced)
1 cup onions (finely minced)

1. Preheat oven to 350 degrees.
2. Combine all ingredients and pour into oiled loaf pan.
3. Cover and bake 50 minutes at 350 degrees.
4. Remove cover and bake 15 minutes longer.
Servings: 12 to 14

Pan-Fried Tofu with Miso Sauce

Try serving this dish with a garnish of julienne-style vegetables.

4 oz. firm-style tofu (sliced into 3 steaks)
oil for frying
Miso Sauce
   2 Tbsp. barley miso
   1 Tbsp. maple syrup
   1 Tbsp. ginger root (minced)
   2 cloves garlic (minced)
   2 tsp. toasted sesame oil

1. In a mixing bowl, combine sauce ingredients, adding a little water if necessary to make a pourable consistency.
2. Place the tofu steaks in a flat dish and pour the sauce over.

3. Marinate at least 1 hour, turning occasionally. Marinate overnight for extra flavor.
4. Pan-fry in an oiled skillet over medium flame. Turn, baste
with additional sauce, and pan-fry the other sides.

Servings: 3

Tofu Fillets

Serve as an entrée garnished with quick-boiled julienne vegetables. Leftover tofu fillets can be cut into small cubes and used in
a stir-fry.

> **16 oz. firm-style tofu (cut crosswise in 8 slices)**
> **3 Tbsp. arrowroot**
> **3 Tbsp. unbleached flour**
> **3 to 4 Tbsp. olive oil**
> **Marinade**
> **¾ cup natural soy sauce**
> **¾ cup sake**
> **2 Tbsp. maple syrup**
> **2 cloves garlic (minced)**
> **2 Tbsp. ginger root (grated)**

1. Combine marinade ingredients in a small mixing bowl and
set aside.
2. Place tofu slices in single layer in pan.
3. Pour marinade over tofu. Poke holes in tofu with fork for better absorption. Let marinate several hours or overnight.
4. Drain tofu and dip in a mixture of arrowroot and flour.
5. Heat oil in a skillet. Sauté fillets slowly until browned on both
sides.

Servings: 8

Tofu Croquettes

Try serving these croquettes with pickles and Dijon-style mustard, or topped with Quick Brown Gravy.

16 oz. tofu

4 oz. package tofu-burger mix

1 cup sunflower seeds

4 Tbsp. sesame seeds (lightly roasted)

2 carrots (grated)

1 tsp. sea salt

2 cups cooked short-grain brown rice

canola oil for frying

1. Combine tofu and tofu-burger mix in a large mixing bowl. Work the tofu-burger mix into the tofu with your hands.
2. Add seeds, carrots, and salt. Combine very well.
3. Add enough rice to make a mixture that will hold its shape.
4. With wet hands, form into croquettes.
5. Preheat skillet and add oil. Pan-fry croquettes until brown on both sides.

Yield: 10 to 12 croquettes

Marinated Tofu

16 oz. firm-style tofu (cut in 6 slices, about 1 inch thick)

3 Tbsp. arrowroot

2 Tbsp. olive oil

Marinade

1 cup natural soy sauce

4 Tbsp. rice vinegar or lemon juice (freshly squeezed)

2 Tbsp. maple syrup

2 Tbsp. toasted sesame oil

3 cloves garlic (minced)

1. Combine marinade ingredients in a flat dish.
2. Place tofu in marinade and place in refrigerator overnight.
3. Drain tofu. Dust with arrowroot and pan-fry in oil until lightly browned on both sides.

Servings: 6

Tofu Stir-Fry

Try serving this over noodles or brown rice.

> **16 oz. firm-style tofu (cut into small cubes)**
> **1 tsp. sesame oil**
> **1 head broccoli (cut into flowerets and lightly steamed)**
> **1 Tbsp. kuzu**
> **Marinade**
> > **4 Tbsp. natural soy sauce**
> > **1 Tbsp. mirin**
> > **1 tsp. maple syrup or barley malt**
> > **¼ tsp. dry ginger**
> > **½ tsp. granulated garlic**
> > **⅓ cup water**

1. Combine marinade ingredients in a small bowl.
2. Place tofu cubes in a flat dish and pour marinade over. Marinate in refrigerator several hours or overnight.
3. Drain tofu cubes and reserve marinade.
4. Heat skillet and add oil. Pan-fry tofu cubes, turning so that they brown on all sides.
5. Add steamed broccoli.
6. Dissolve kuzu in reserved marinade.
7. Stir kuzu mixture into skillet and heat through.

Yield: 6 to 8

Tempeh Sauerkraut

Great served over brown rice or noodles.

> **4 to 5 cups water**
> **1 tsp. sea salt**
> **8 oz. tempeh**
> **1 Tbsp. olive oil**
> **2 cloves garlic (minced)**
> **2 cups fresh mushrooms (thinly sliced)**
> **1 Tbsp. natural soy sauce**
> **1 Tbsp. natural sauerkraut**
> **2 scallions (thinly sliced)**

1. Bring water to a boil. Add salt and tempeh. Cover and cook 30 minutes.
2. Drain tempeh and chop finely.
3. Heat a skillet over medium flame. Add oil, garlic, and mushrooms. Sauté until mushrooms begin to give off liquid.
4. Add tempeh, soy sauce, and sauerkraut. Cover and simmer gently 5 to 10 minutes.
5. Garnish with scallions when serving.

Servings: 4 or 5

Teriyaki Tempeh

Great served over noodles or whole grain, or placed on wooden skewers and served as shish kabobs.

> 8 oz. tempeh (cubed)
> 1 or 2 cups oil, for deep-frying
> 3 cups boiling water
> **Teriyaki Sauce**
> 2 onions (chopped)
> 2 cloves garlic (minced)
> 1 Tbsp. oil, for sautéing
> 1/2 cup water
> 2 Tbsp. natural soy sauce
> 1 1/2 Tbsp. mirin or sake
> 1 Tbsp. maple syrup
> 1/2 tsp. ginger root (grated)
> 1/4 tsp. dry mustard

1. To make teriyaki sauce, sauté onions and garlic in oil for 3 minutes.
2. Add 1/2 cup water. Cover and simmer until onions are soft.
3. Add remaining sauce ingredients. Heat through.
4. Deep-fry tempeh and drain on paper towels to remove oil.
5. To further reduce oil, dip deep-fried tempeh in the boiling water and remove to a colander to drain.
6. Stir tempeh into the teriyaki sauce and simmer a few minutes to blend flavors.

Servings: 6

Broccoli Quiche

The secret of this recipe is to cook the onions in step one until they are completely transparent and soft. This makes a sweet-tasting filling.

> 2 Tbsp. olive oil
> 5 cups onions (chopped)
> ¾ tsp. sea salt
> ½ tsp. granulated garlic
> 3 cups carrots (shredded)
> 3 cups butternut squash (shredded)
> 10 oz. tofu (blended smoothly)
> 1½ cups broccoli flowerets (steamed)
> 2 Rolled Pie Crusts, page 185 (baked about 10 minutes)

1. Heat a heavy pot and add oil. Add onions and salt. Cover and sauté about 45 minutes over very low flame. (Sautéing the onions with salt brings out the juice and prevents sticking.)
2. Preheat oven to 350 degrees.
3. Add garlic, carrot, and squash to onions. Cover and continue to cook until vegetables are soft, about 10 minutes.
4. Add blended tofu and heat through.
5. Transfer a quarter of the tofu mixture to each pie shell. Place half the broccoli in a layer over the tofu mixture in each pie shell. Cover with remaining tofu mixture.
6. Bake uncovered at 350 degrees for 1 hour.

Yield: 2 quiches

Vegetable Noodle Bake

What a winner! This is one of my favorite entrées. Try making it for your next potluck. The secret of this dish is slow-cooking the onions. The onions become very sweet when cooked in this manner.

> **2 Tbsp. corn oil**
> **8 cups onions (chopped)**
> **1 tsp. sea salt**
> **2 cups carrot (grated)**
> **2 cups butternut squash (peeled and grated)**
> **3 cloves garlic (minced)**
> **10 oz. firm-style tofu**
> **10 oz. udon noodles (cooked and drained)**

1. Heat a large heavy pot and add oil.
2. Add onions and salt. Cover and sauté for 45 minutes over very low flame.
3. When onions are very soft, add carrots, squash, and garlic. Cover and continue to sauté until vegetables are tender, about 15 minutes.
4. Preheat oven to 350 degrees.
5. In a blender or food processor, blend tofu until smooth, adding 1 or 2 tablespoons water, if necessary, to make a smooth consistency.
6. Stir tofu into vegetable mixture and combine very well. Cook for 5 to 10 minutes to heat through.
7. Oil a 9x12-inch baking dish. Combine cooked noodles with vegetable sauce and press into baking dish. Cover and bake at 350 degrees for 45 minutes.
8. Remove cover and bake 5 minutes longer.
9. Cut into squares and serve.

Servings: 9

Vegetable Pot Pie

2 cups water
½ cup cashews or sunflower seeds
¼ tsp. sea salt
½ tsp. dried thyme, or your favorite herbal blend
2 tsp. granulated onion
2 Tbsp. kuzu, dissolved in 2 Tbsp. water
1 carrot (finely diced)
1 cup fresh corn (kernels cut from cob)
1 cup yellow squash (finely diced)
½ cup broccoli (finely chopped)
1 Rolled Pie Crust, page 185 (baked)

1. Blend the first 5 ingredients in a food processor until smooth.
2. Transfer mixture to a saucepan and bring to a simmer.
3. Stir in kuzu mixture and stir until thickened.
4. In a separate pot, steam all vegetables until tender.
5. Combine vegetables with sauce and spoon into the pie shell.
6. Serve while warm.

Servings: 6 to 8

Vegetable Pie

This entrée has a naturally sweet flavor.

> **4 cups onions (coarsely chopped)**
> **2 Tbsp. olive oil**
> **¾ tsp. sea salt**
> **2 cups carrots (shredded)**
> **1 cup butternut squash (shredded)**
> **½ tsp. granulated garlic**
> **1 cup sunflower seeds (ground in blender)**
> **3 Tbsp. cooked brown rice**
> **1 Rolled Pie Crust, page 185 (baked 10 minutes)**

1. Preheat oven to 350 degrees.
2. Sauté onions in oil about 5 minutes.
3. Add salt. Cover and cook over very low flame about 1 hour.
4. Stir in carrots and squash. Cover and cook another 10 to 15 minutes, or until vegetables are tender.
5. Stir in garlic, seeds, and rice. Set aside to cool slightly.
6. Transfer mixture to pie shell.
7. Bake uncovered at 350 degrees for 50 minutes.

Servings: 8

Fish

Before I began following a macrobiotic diet I was weak, easily fatigued, unfocused, undirected, and even lost. I was encouraged to eat a balanced diet that included more yang foods such as whole grains and small amounts of fish. Within a few weeks of beginning this diet I felt stronger and more focused. My underlying abilities came to the surface and I became much more goal-oriented. I had long-lasting energy; I also felt more powerful and self-confident. Changing my diet changed my condition and restored my sense of inner strength.

Fish provides us with a wealth of gifts. In addition to its strength-giving qualities, it is a nutritionally rich food, containing plenty of protein, iron, calcium and other nutrients. Most white fish also contain omega-3 polyunsaturated fats, which lower cholesterol and protect against heart disease. White fish, especially, are low in fat and cholesterol. Fish is a good food, and once you learn how to prepare it properly, your family will come to love its taste and strength-giving benefits.

Baked Halibut with Vegetables

> 2 halibut fillets, 6 to 8 oz. per fillet
> 2 carrots (minced)
> 2 ribs celery (minced)
> 1 bunch scallions (sliced)
> 1 Tbsp. lemon juice (freshly squeezed)
> 1/2 tsp. sea salt
> 3 Tbsp. sesame oil

1. Preheat oven to 350 degrees.
2. Arrange fillets in baking pan. Spread vegetables over fish.

3. Combine lemon juice, salt, and oil in a small bowl.
4. Sprinkle lemon mixture over fish. Cover tightly and bake 25 minutes or until fish is tender.

Servings: 2

Baked Fish Fillet with Fruit Sauce

> 1 cup vegetable broth
> 1 Tbsp. natural soy sauce
> 2 tsp. kuzu
> $\frac{1}{2}$ cup raisins
> 2 Tbsp. celery (thinly sliced)
> $1\frac{1}{3}$ cups boiling water
> $\frac{2}{3}$ cup couscous
> 2 Tbsp. parsley (chopped)
> $\frac{1}{4}$ tsp. sea salt
> 2 Tbsp. sesame oil
> 4 orange roughy fillets, 6 to 8 oz. per fillet
> 1 Tbsp. natural soy sauce

1. Preheat oven to 450 degrees.
2. To make fruit sauce, whisk broth, soy sauce, and kuzu in a small saucepan. Bring to a boil and add raisins and celery.
3. Cook and stir until thickened. Simmer gently 2 minutes more. Keep warm.
4. Stir together the boiling water, couscous, parsley, and salt in a mixing bowl. Cover and let stand 5 minutes.
5. Place fish fillets in an oiled baking dish. Brush fish with 1 tablespoon soy sauce.
6. Bake at 450 degrees until fish is tender (about 5 minutes per $\frac{1}{2}$-inch thickness of fish).
7. Remove cover from couscous and fluff with a fork.
8. To serve, place a bed of couscous on serving plate. Place a fillet atop couscous. Ladle fruit sauce over fish.

Servings: 4

Baked Salmon Steaks

2 salmon steaks, 6 to 8 oz. per steak
3 Tbsp. oil
1 tsp. natural Worcestershire-style sauce
1 tsp. onion (grated)
½ tsp. sea salt

1. Preheat oven to 350 degrees.
2. Place salmon steaks in an oiled shallow baking pan.
3. To make a sauce, combine remaining ingredients with a whisk in a small mixing bowl.
4. Brush sauce lightly on salmon.
5. Bake approximately 25 to 30 minutes at 350 degrees.

Servings: 2

Broiled Halibut Steaks

4 halibut steaks, 6 to 8 oz. per steak
4 lemon slices
Marinade
3 Tbsp. natural soy sauce
2 Tbsp. rice syrup
1 tsp. ground ginger
½ tsp. granulated garlic
1 tsp. lemon peel (grated)
¼ cup lemon juice (freshly squeezed)
¼ cup water

1. Arrange fish in a shallow dish.
2. Combine marinade ingredients in a small mixing bowl.
3. Pour marinade over fish. Cover and refrigerate 1 hour.
4. Set oven control to broil.
5. Arrange steaks on broiler rack. Broil steaks 3 inches from heat about 5 minutes.

6. Turn fish and brush the other sides with marinade. Broil 5 minutes or until fish flakes easily with a fork.
7. Serve garnished with lemon slices.
Servings: 4

Broiled Orange Roughy Fillets

Good served with a salad of romaine lettuce, red radishes, cucumbers, and celery, with Lemon Soy Dressing.

4 orange roughy fillets, 6 to 8 oz. per fillet
3 Tbsp. olive oil
2 cloves garlic (minced)
¹/₂ tsp. sea salt
2 Tbsp. lemon juice (freshly squeezed)

1. Preheat broiler.
2. Place fish in an oiled pan.
3. Combine remaining ingredients in a blender and process until smooth.
4. Spread half of the mixture over fish. Broil 8 minutes.
5. Turn fish and spread with remaining mixture and broil approximately 8 minutes, or until done.
Servings: 4

Pan-Fried Orange Roughy with Miso =

Sole fillets may be used in place of orange roughy.

> **2 orange roughy fillets, 6 to 8 oz. per fillet**
> **3 Tbsp. natural soy sauce**
> **½ cup mellow white miso**
> **4 Tbsp. water**
> **2 Tbsp. rice syrup**
> **1 tsp. ginger juice (squeezed from grated fresh ginger root)**
> **2 Tbsp. sesame oil**
> **2 scallions (thinly sliced)**

1. Rinse and dry fish fillets.
2. Combine soy sauce, miso, water, rice syrup, and ginger juice. Marinate fish in this mixture while preparing skillet.
3. Heat a large skillet and add sesame oil.
4. Pan-fry fish on one side. Turn fish over and brush with additional marinade.
5. Cover skillet and steam 3 to 4 minutes over low flame.
6. Serve immediately garnished with scallions.

Servings: 2

Orange Roughy Fillet with Sweet Mustard Topping

> **2 Tbsp. Dijon-style mustard**
> **2 tsp. garlic (minced)**
> **2 tsp. lemon juice (freshly squeezed)**
> **1 Tbsp. maple syrup**
> **2 Tbsp. sesame oil**
> **2 orange roughy fillets, 6 to 8 oz. per fillet**

1. To make mustard topping, combine first 4 ingredients in a

small bowl.
2. Heat a skillet and add sesame oil.
3. Place fish fillets in skillet and brown on one side.
4. Turn fillets over and brush mustard topping on the fillets.
5. Place lid on skillet. Turn flame off and leave covered 5 minutes so that steam captured in skillet will finish cooking the fillets.
6. Turn fish again and brush topping on other side. Serve immediately.
Servings: 2

Red Snapper in Miso Mustard Sauce

2 red snapper fillets, 6 to 8 oz. per fillet
cornmeal
2 Tbsp. olive oil
2 Tbsp. fresh ginger root (minced)
2 cloves garlic (minced)
Miso Mustard Sauce
2 Tbsp. mellow white miso
2 tsp. Dijon-style mustard
2 tsp. mirin
1 Tbsp. brown-rice syrup
3 Tbsp. water

1. Rinse and wipe fillets dry. Dust with cornmeal.
2. Heat skillet and add olive oil. Sauté ginger and garlic briefly.
3. Add fish fillets to skillet and brown 2 minutes on each side.
4. Combine sauce ingredients in a mixing bowl and pour over fish. Cover skillet and simmer 1 minute.
5. Turn off flame and leave skillet covered for 1 or 2 minutes before serving.
Servings: 2

Salmon Rice Croquettes

An old-time macrobiotic teacher arrived at the center and gave a lecture. We had planned to go out afterward but by the time I finished closing he had become interested in a movie on a little TV in the kitchen. He said, "Let's just stay and watch this movie." I said, "If you're going to do that, I'm going to cook." I found some red sockeye salmon and combined it with rice, scallion, and lemon. "Salmon?" he laughed. He ate three-quarters of it. And that's how my salmon rice croquettes came about.

> 1 lb. canned red sockeye salmon
> 1 tsp. lemon juice (freshly squeezed)
> 1 to 2 Tbsp. unbleached flour
> 1 cup freshly-cooked short-grain brown rice
> 1 scallion (minced)
> ½ tsp. sea salt
> Sweet and Sour Red Cabbage, page 51

1. Drain salmon, remove bones, and break into small pieces.
2. Combine salmon, lemon juice, flour, rice, scallion, and salt.
3. Shape croquettes by placing a tablespoon of the mixture in the palm of the hand and molding it.
4. Pan-fry in hot, oiled skillet.
5. Serve with sweet and sour red cabbage on the side.

Yield: 10 to 12 croquettes

Fish Soup

Try adding other ingredients such as leeks, parsnips, kale, Brussels sprouts, or burdock or season with an herb such as thyme or rosemary. Serve in individual bowls garnished with parsley or scallions.

> 2 Tbsp. sesame oil
> 2 onions (chopped)

1 carrot (cubed)
¹/₂ head cabbage (cut in chunks)
water to cover
1 slice fresh ginger root
2 to 3 tsp. natural soy sauce, or to taste
10 to 12 oz. whitefish (cut in bite-sized pieces)

1. Heat pot and add oil.
2. Place a layer of onions in bottom of pot. Layer carrots and cabbage over onions.
3. Add enough water to cover vegetables and bring to a boil.
4. Add ginger root and 1 teaspoon soy sauce.
5. Reduce flame. Cover and simmer 20 minutes, or until vegetables are tender.
6. Add fish. Cover and simmer 8 to 10 minutes or until fish is tender.
7. Taste and season with additional soy sauce, if desired.

Servings: 3 or 4

Poached Fish

water
¹/₂ tsp. sea salt
1 onion (sliced)
3 slices lemon
3 sprigs fresh parsley
1 bay leaf
2 fish fillets, 6 to 8 oz. per fillet

1. Place 1¹/₂ inches water in a large skillet. Add salt and a bouquet garni of the onion, lemon, parsley, and bay leaf.
2. Arrange fish in a single layer in skillet.
3. Cover tightly and simmer 5 minutes or until fish is tender.
4. Remove fish to a serving platter and discard bouquet garni.

Servings: 2

=Sauces and Dressings=

A delicious sauce sometimes makes the difference between a good meal and a great one. A good sauce brings everything to life. It moistens and enriches your food. It makes the flavors of your dish more accessible to your palate. It makes your meal more sensuous.

The average restaurant or homemade sauce or gravy is made from flour and grease, and often chemicals and preservatives. It's no good for you and does little for the food. It buries your dish in fat. My sauces and gravies are rich in flavor and bring out the best in the meal itself. And they're healthful.

The average prepared dressing contains a large amount of fat, sugar, artificial flavors, and chemical additives. The dressings presented in this book are made with the highest-quality natural ingredients in order to benefit health.

I use a wide assortment of bases, such as whole-wheat pastry flour, tofu, and tahini. I like to use a variety of misos because there are so many flavors and different types. I also use umeboshi and rice vinegars, soy sauce, herbs, and spices. Often, I sauté some onions until they are soft and translucent, then add them to the sauce. I love garlic, basil, and other herbs, which fill the kitchen with wonderful aromas and enhance the flavors of the dish. Sometimes I add kuzu, a tasteless herb that traditional healers use to help strengthen the intestines. Kuzu thickens any liquid and gives sauces a creamy texture. It is a wonderful base for puddings or creamy desserts, too.

As you soon will see, there are many delicious and luscious sauces, gravies, dressings, and spreads for you to choose from. In my restaurant, I offered a couple of different sauces daily. People loved them. I hope you will, too.

Cashew "Cheese" Sauce

This "cheese" sauce may be served over bean dishes, burritos, or chalupas. I like to cook macaroni and combine it with Cashew "Cheese" Sauce for an old favorite "macaroni and cheese" dish.

$\frac{1}{2}$ cup water

$\frac{1}{3}$ cup lemon juice (freshly squeezed)

4 oz. jar pimentos

$\frac{2}{3}$ cup cashews

3 Tbsp. nutritional-yeast flakes

2 Tbsp. sesame seeds

1 tsp. onion salt

$\frac{1}{4}$ tsp. granulated garlic

$\frac{1}{4}$ cup safflower or canola oil

1. Place all ingredients except oil in blender or food processor.
2. Blend at high speed until creamy smooth.
3. Stop blender and push food down from sides with a spatula. (Add 1 tablespoon water if too dry.)
4. Slowly add oil while blending at high speed.
5. Transfer mixture to a saucepan and heat through.

Yield: $1\frac{2}{3}$ cups

Chinese Stir-Fry Sauce

Add this sauce to vegetables that have been stir-fried three or four minutes in an oiled skillet. Heat through. Great served over noodles or grain.

> 6 Tbsp. rice vinegar
> 6 Tbsp. maple syrup or barley malt
> 3/4 cup water
> 2 Tbsp. natural soy sauce
> 1 Tbsp. kuzu, dissolved in 1 Tbsp. water
> 1 Tbsp. ginger root (minced)

1. Place first 4 ingredients in a small saucepan. Bring to a boil.
2. Stir kuzu mixture into sauce. Cook until clear and thickened.
3. Turn flame off and stir in ginger.

Yield: 1½ cups

Cranberry Sauce

> 1 cup raisins
> 1 cup apple juice
> 4 Tbsp. kanten flakes
> 2½ cups orange juice (freshly squeezed)
> 1 Tbsp. maple syrup
> 2 cups cranberries
> pinch sea salt
> 2 Tbsp. kuzu, dissolved in 2 Tbsp. water

1. Simmer raisins in apple juice for 5 minutes.
2. Dissolve kanten flakes in orange juice and add to simmering pot.
3. Stir in maple syrup, cranberries, and salt. Simmer 10 minutes.
4. Add kuzu mixture. Simmer 2 minutes.
5. Pour into a bowl and chill before serving.

Yield: 3¾ cups

Ginger Sauce

Try serving this sauce over Millet "Meatballs" or Tofu Croquettes.

> 1 cup cashews
> 2 cups water
> 2 tsp. canola oil
> 2 Tbsp. ginger root (grated)
> 2 Tbsp. unbleached flour
> 2 tsp. natural soy sauce
> 1/2 tsp. sea salt

1. Place cashews and 1 cup water in blender. Purée until creamy smooth. Let blender run until all cashews have blended smoothly.
2. Transfer mixture to a mixing bowl. Add remaining 1 cup water and stir well to make cashew milk.
3. Heat a saucepan and add canola oil. Sauté ginger for 1 minute.
4. Add flour and cook over low flame, stirring, for 2 minutes.
5. Slowly add cashew milk while stirring with a wire whisk. Bring to a boil, stirring constantly to avoid lumps.
6. When mixture thickens, add soy sauce and salt.

Yield: 3 cups

Gourmet White Sauce

Great over Lentil Loaf or greens.

>2 cups water
>½ cup cashews
>2 Tbsp. arrowroot
>2 tsp. granulated onion
>2 Tbsp. corn oil
>½ tsp. sea salt

1. Blend all ingredients in a blender.
2. Transfer to a saucepan and cook, stirring constantly, until thickened.

Yield: 2 cups

Miso Scallion Sauce

Try this sauce over millet or rice for a special treat.

>2 tsp. sesame oil
>1 bunch scallions (thinly sliced)
>2 tsp. barley miso
>⅓ cup water

1. Heat pan. Add oil and scallions.
2. Stir gently over medium flame for 2 minutes.
3. Purée miso in water and add to scallions.
4. Reduce flame to low. Cover and simmer gently about 5 minutes.

Yield: ⅓ cup

Miso Sesame Dipping Sauce

I often serve this sauce with lightly steamed vegetables.

> 2 Tbsp. brown-rice miso
> 1 Tbsp. maple syrup
> 1 tsp. garlic (minced)
> 2 tsp. ginger juice (squeezed from grated fresh ginger root)
> 1 tsp. toasted sesame oil

1. Combine all ingredients with a whisk until smooth.
2. Transfer to a saucepan and heat through.

Yield: 1/4 cup

Miso Tahini Sauce with a Twist

This sauce is good served over udon or soba noodles.

> 1 cup raw sesame tahini
> 1/4 cup mellow white miso
> 2 Tbsp. natural soy sauce
> 1 Tbsp. rice vinegar
> 1 1/2 tsp. ginger root (grated)
> 2 cloves garlic (minced)
> water as needed to blend

1. Blend all ingredients in a blender until creamy smooth.
2. Transfer to a saucepan and heat through.

Yield: 1 1/2 cups

Quick Dill Cucumber Sauce

This sauce is great with steamed vegetables.

> **1 cucumber (peeled and seeded)**
> **2 cloves garlic (minced)**
> **1 Tbsp. lemon juice (freshly squeezed)**
> **2 Tbsp. rice vinegar**
> **2 Tbsp. maple syrup or other sweetener**
> **1 Tbsp. raw sesame tahini**
> **1 Tbsp. dried dill weed**
> **½ cup soy milk**

1. Place all ingredients in blender and purée until smooth.
Yield: 1 cup

Spinach Pesto

This sauce can be served over noodles or steamed vegetables.

> **1 bunch spinach**
> **5 tsp. mellow white miso**
> **2 cloves garlic (minced)**
> **½ cup walnuts (chopped)**
> **4 Tbsp. olive oil**
> **1 Tbsp. water, if needed**

1. Combine all ingredients in a food processor and purée until
   smooth.
Yield: 1¼ cups

Sweet and Sour Sauce

Fantastic served over grilled tempeh, tofu, or seitan.

1¾ cups apple juice
2 Tbsp. maple syrup
2 Tbsp. rice vinegar
3 Tbsp. rice miso
2 tsp. dry ginger
1 Tbsp. kuzu or 2 Tbsp. arrowroot, dissolved in 1 Tbsp.
   water

1. Combine first 5 ingredients in a saucepan. Bring to a simmer.
2. Add kuzu or arrowroot mixture to saucepan, using a whisk to combine.
3. Stir until sauce begins to thicken.

Yield: 2 cups

Sweet Squash Sauce

2 onions (diced)
2 cups butternut squash (peeled and cubed)
¾ to 1 cup water
¼ tsp. sea salt
½ tsp. ginger juice (squeezed from grated fresh ginger
   root)
1 tsp. kuzu, dissolved in 1 Tbsp. water

1. Place onions in a heavy 2-quart pot. Layer squash on top of onions. Add water and salt.
2. Cover and bring to a boil over medium-high flame.
3. Reduce flame to low. Cover and simmer 40 minutes or until vegetables are tender.
4. Add ginger juice and dissolved kuzu to vegetables, stirring until thickened, about 2 or 3 minutes.

Yield: 2 cups

Tofu "Sour Cream"

Try tofu "sour cream" over Mexican Chalupas or steamed vegetables.

> 8 oz. firm-style tofu
> 4 Tbsp. lemon juice (freshly squeezed)
> 2 Tbsp. canola oil
> 1 Tbsp. mellow white miso
> ½ tsp. Dijon-style mustard
> 1 tsp. sea salt
> 2 or 3 Tbsp. water

1. Combine all ingredients in food processor and purée until smooth.

Yield: 1½ cups

Very Good Brown Sauce

Turn your loaves and croquettes into gourmet affairs with this sauce.

> 1 cup vegetable stock or water
> 4 to 5 tsp. arrowroot
> ½ tsp. maple syrup
> ½ tsp. toasted sesame oil
> 2 Tbsp. natural soy sauce

1. Combine all ingredients in saucepan.
2. Bring to a boil, stirring constantly. Cook 2 minutes or until thickened.

Yield: 1 cup

Vinaigrette Sauce

Great served over Quick Boiled Vegetables or garden salad.

> ½ cup canola oil
> ¼ cup apple-cider vinegar
> 3 Tbsp. sweet pickle relish
> 1 tsp. sea salt
> 2 tsp. barley malt

1. Blend all ingredients in a blender for 1 minute at low speed.
Yield: ¾ cup

White Sauce

To use this sauce in the Scalloped Cauliflower dish, use one tablespoon mellow white miso instead of the sea salt.

> 3 Tbsp. corn oil
> 3 Tbsp. unbleached flour
> 1 cup vegetable stock or water
> ¾ tsp. sea salt, or 1 Tbsp. soy sauce

1. Heat oil in skillet. Add flour and cook over low flame, stirring constantly, for 2 minutes.
2. Slowly add the stock and salt.
3. Cook over medium flame, stirring, for 3 to 4 minutes or until sauce thickens.
4. Reduce flame to low and simmer 5 minutes.
Yield: 1¼ cups

Brown Gravy

4 oz. tofu (mashed)
8 oz. natural brown-gravy mix
1½ cups water
½ cup mushrooms (sliced and sautéed)
soy sauce, optional

1. Combine first 3 ingredients in a blender and purée until smooth.
2. Transfer to a saucepan. Simmer until thickened.
3. Stir in mushrooms.
4. Taste and adjust seasoning, adding soy sauce if needed.
Yield: 2 cups

Quick Brown Gravy

Try serving this gravy atop grains or croquettes.

2 cups soy milk
2 to 3 Tbsp. arrowroot
½ tsp. sea salt
2 tsp. granulated onion
2 Tbsp. canola oil
3 Tbsp. natural soy sauce

1. Blend all ingredients in blender or food processor.
2. Transfer to a saucepan and heat, stirring constantly, until thickened.
Yield: 2¼ cups

Chicken-Style Gravy

Great served over Rice Walnut Loaf.

> 1/2 cup cashews
> 2 Tbsp. arrowroot
> 1/4 tsp. dried sage
> 1/8 tsp. dried thyme
> 1/2 tsp. celery salt
> 1 tsp. granulated onion
> 1/4 tsp. granulated garlic
> 2 tsp. sea salt
> 3/4 cup water
> 2 cups water

1. Blend all ingredients, except 2 cups water, until smooth and creamy.
2. Bring 2 cups water to a boil.
3. Add blended ingredients, stirring until mixture begins to boil.

Yield: 2¾ cups

Easy Cashew Gravy

I serve this gravy over grains or croquettes.

> 1/2 cup cashew butter
> 2 1/4 cups water
> 2 Tbsp. safflower oil
> 3 Tbsp. onion (chopped)
> 2 Tbsp. whole-wheat pastry flour
> 1 Tbsp. kuzu
> 1 tsp. sea salt

1. Blend all ingredients in a blender until smooth.
2. Transfer to a saucepan and heat until thick.

Yield: 2 cups

Mushroom Kuzu Gravy

2 cups water or vegetable stock
4 Tbsp. natural soy sauce
8 oz. mushrooms (sliced)
2 Tbsp. kuzu, dissolved in 2 Tbsp. water

1. Combine water and soy sauce in a small saucepan.
2. Bring to a boil and add mushrooms. Reduce flame and simmer 2 minutes.
3. Stir in dissolved kuzu and stir until thickened.

Yield: 2¹/₂ cups

Old-Fashioned Mushroom Gravy

1 onion (chopped)
2 cups mushrooms (sliced)
2 Tbsp. corn oil
3 Tbsp. unbleached flour
1 cup vegetable stock or water
¹/₂ tsp. sea salt
2 Tbsp. natural soy sauce
¹/₂ tsp. dried basil, dried thyme, or other dried herb, optional

1. Sauté onion and mushrooms in oil until onion is soft, about 10 minutes.
2. Combine flour and stock or water in a separate bowl. Beat with a whisk to make a smooth mixture.
3. Gradually pour the flour mixture into the mushroom mixture and cook until thickened.
4. Add salt, soy sauce, and if desired, dried herb of your choice.
5. Simmer gently, stirring constantly, for 5 minutes.

Yield: 2¹/₂ cups

Onion Gravy

1 Tbsp. sesame oil
1 cup onions (sliced)
$\frac{1}{4}$ tsp. sea salt, or to taste
1 cup water
2 tsp. kuzu, dissolved in 1 Tbsp. water

1. Heat skillet and add oil.
2. Add onions and salt. Cover and sauté over very low flame until transparent and tender, about 20 minutes.
3. Add water and bring to a boil. Whisk in dissolved kuzu.
4. Adjust seasoning, adding a little more salt if needed.

Yield: 1$\frac{1}{4}$ cups

Zippy Onion Gravy

In Texas, we call this "Panhandle Gravy."

1 onion (minced)
2 Tbsp. sesame oil
2 Tbsp. whole-wheat pastry flour
1 cup vegetable stock or water
$\frac{1}{2}$ tsp. sea salt
$\frac{1}{8}$ tsp. white pepper
$\frac{1}{2}$ tsp. natural Worcestershire-style sauce, optional

1. Sauté onion in oil for 5 minutes.
2. Cover and simmer over low flame 10 minutes, stirring occasionally.
3. Blend in flour and cook until flour turns brown, stirring constantly.
4. Add stock slowly, stirring constantly.
5. Add salt and pepper. Cook until thickened.
6. Add Worcestershire sauce to give extra zip.

Yield: 1$\frac{1}{4}$ cups

Savory Miso Gravy

Try this gravy over Tofu Croquettes or any loaf or burger.

2 onions (sliced in lengthwise crescents)
1 Tbsp. sesame oil
1 cup water
1 Tbsp. kuzu
2 Tbsp. mellow white miso
¾ cup water
¼ tsp. sea salt, optional

1. Sauté onions in oil until transparent.
2. Add 1 cup water and simmer 20 minutes.
3. Dissolve kuzu and miso in the ¾ cup water and stir into onion mixture.
4. When gravy thickens, simmer 1 minute more.
5. Taste and add salt if desired.

Yield: 2 cups

All-Purpose Vinaigrette Dressing

This dressing can be used on any green salad or steamed greens, such as kale or collards. Just a drizzle is all that's needed. It will keep up to one week in the refrigerator.

1 Tbsp. shallots or onion (minced)
1 Tbsp. Dijon-style mustard
3 Tbsp. apple-cider vinegar
½ tsp. sea salt
½ cup extra-virgin olive oil

1. In a small mixing bowl, combine all ingredients.
2. Use a wire whisk to blend well.

Yield: ⅔ cup

Celery Seed Dressing

When you're tired of the taste of vegetables, try this dressing and make them come alive in your mouth. I like this dressing on any vegetable or leafy salad.

2 Tbsp. apple-cider vinegar
¾ tsp. dry mustard
5 Tbsp. maple syrup
½ tsp. sea salt
½ cup extra-virgin olive oil
1 tsp. celery seeds

1. Place first 4 ingredients in a blender.
2. Gradually add the olive oil while the blender is running.
3. Turn the blender off and stir in celery seeds.
4. Chill before serving.

Yield: ¾ cup

Creamy Lemon Dressing

Good with steamed vegetables or raw salad.

¼ cup canola oil
2 Tbsp. lemon juice (freshly squeezed)
1 Tbsp. natural soy sauce
¼ cup tofu mayonnaise

1. Combine all ingredients in a bowl, using a wire whisk.

Yield: ⅔ cup

Elegant Sesame Dressing

Get ready for compliments when you serve this dressing. Try it with steamed broccoli, cauliflower, Brussels sprouts, or cooked greens.

> **8 oz. firm-style tofu**
> **1/2 cup water**
> **1/4 cup sesame oil**
> **1 Tbsp. toasted sesame oil**
> **2 1/2 Tbsp. rice vinegar**
> **4 Tbsp. mellow white miso**
> **2 cloves garlic (minced)**
> **2 Tbsp. rice syrup or 1 Tbsp. maple syrup**

1. Combine all ingredients in a blender until creamy smooth.
Yield: 1 3/4 cups

Herbed Tofu Dressing

> **8 oz. firm-style tofu**
> **1/2 cup extra-virgin olive oil**
> **1/2 cup water**
> **1/3 cup apple-cider vinegar or rice vinegar**
> **1 Tbsp. Dijon-style mustard**
> **1/2 tsp. basil**
> **1/2 tsp. oregano**
> **1 clove garlic (chopped)**
> **4 Tbsp. onion (chopped)**
> **1 tsp. sea salt**

1. Combine all ingredients in a food processor.
2. Blend until creamy smooth.
Yield: 2 1/3 cups

Lemon Sesame Dressing

Try this dressing over Quick Boiled Vegetables.

> 3 Tbsp. natural soy sauce
> 1/2 cup water
> 1 Tbsp. lemon juice (freshly squeezed)
> 1/4 tsp. toasted sesame oil

1. Combine all ingredients and mix well.
Yield: 3/4 cup

Lemon Soy Dressing

Great served over steamed vegetables or salad.

> 4 Tbsp. extra-virgin olive oil
> 1 Tbsp. natural soy sauce
> 3 Tbsp. lemon juice (freshly squeezed)

1. Combine all ingredients.
Yield: 1/2 cup

Mustard Vinaigrette

This dressing keeps well for one week in a glass jar in the refrigerator. Very good on raw salads or Quick Boiled Vegetables.

> 1/2 cup extra-virgin olive oil
> 1/2 cup apple-cider vinegar
> 4 Tbsp. onion (minced)
> 1/2 tsp. dry mustard
> 2 tsp. maple syrup or barley malt
> 1/2 tsp. sea salt

1. Blend all ingredients in a blender or food processor until smooth.
Yield: 1 cup

Miso Dressing

Super served over fresh or steamed vegetables.

> 3 Tbsp. mellow white miso
> 1 Tbsp. rice vinegar
> 1 Tbsp. rice syrup
> 1/2 tsp. toasted sesame oil
> 1/2 tsp. lemon juice (freshly squeezed)
> 4 Tbsp. water

1. Combine all ingredients thoroughly.

Yield: 1/2 cup

Miso Ginger Dressing

> 1/2 cup canola oil
> 3 Tbsp. brown-rice vinegar
> 4 Tbsp. brown-rice miso
> 1/2 tsp. toasted sesame oil
> 1/4 tsp. dry mustard
> 1/2 tsp. ginger juice (squeezed from grated fresh ginger root)
> 1 clove garlic (minced)

1. Combine all ingredients in blender and blend until smooth.

Yield: 3/4 cup

Sesame Garlic Dressing

I have served this dressing over everything from grains to hiji-ki. It is special!

$\frac{1}{4}$ cup raw sesame tahini
$\frac{3}{4}$ cup water
4 Tbsp. natural soy sauce
1 Tbsp. toasted sesame oil
1 Tbsp. maple syrup
1 Tbsp. rice vinegar
4 cloves garlic (minced)

1. Place all ingredients in blender or food processor and purée until smooth.

Yield: 1$\frac{1}{4}$ cups

Soy Vinaigrette

I like to marinate tofu slices in this sauce for several hours and then pan-fry them.

2 Tbsp. natural soy sauce
1 Tbsp. sesame oil
1 Tbsp. rice vinegar
1 Tbsp. mirin
1 Tbsp. lemon juice (freshly squeezed)
1$\frac{1}{2}$ tsp. maple syrup
1 tsp. fresh ginger root (grated)
1 tsp. toasted sesame oil
1 garlic clove (minced)

1. Whisk all ingredients together in a small bowl.

Yield: $\frac{1}{2}$ cup

Smooth Vinaigrette Dressing

Use this dressing to jazz up pasta salads or try it on lightly cooked greens.

> ¼ cup extra-virgin olive oil
> 1 Tbsp. natural soy sauce
> 1 Tbsp. brown-rice vinegar
> 1 Tbsp. lemon juice (freshly squeezed)
> 3 Tbsp. maple syrup
> 1 Tbsp. water
> 2 cloves garlic (minced)

1. Combine all ingredients in a blender and purée until smooth.
Yield: ¾ cup

Spicy Tofu Dip

Try serving this with lightly steamed vegetables for dipping.

> 8 oz. firm-style tofu
> 2 Tbsp. canola oil
> 2 Tbsp. lemon juice (freshly squeezed)
> 1 Tbsp. water
> 1 tsp. Dijon-style mustard
> 1 tsp. maple syrup

1. Blend all ingredients until creamy smooth.
Yield: 1¼ cups

Tofu Dressing

8 oz. firm-style tofu
4 Tbsp. olive oil
2 tsp. maple syrup or barley malt
2 Tbsp. apple-cider vinegar
1 tsp. sea salt
1 tsp. onion (chopped)
½ tsp. granulated garlic
3 Tbsp. sweet pickle relish
1 tsp. Italian seasoning

1. Combine first 6 ingredients in a blender and purée.
2. Transfer to a mixing bowl. Stir in remaining ingredients.
Yield: 1½ cups

Tofu Italian Dressing

For a different taste, try one tablespoon dried dill weed in place of the Italian seasoning.

16 oz. tofu
2 cups tofu mayonnaise
½ cup brown-rice vinegar or apple-cider vinegar
1½ cups water
1 Tbsp. granulated garlic
1 Tbsp. Italian seasoning
2 tsp. sea salt

1. Place all ingredients in a food processor and blend until creamy smooth.
Yield: 6 cups

Tofu Salad Dressing

This dressing will keep four or five days in a glass jar in the refrigerator.

> 12 to 14 oz. firm-style tofu
> ¼ cup canola oil
> ¼ cup lemon juice (freshly squeezed)
> 1 tsp. sea salt
> 2 tsp. maple syrup
> 1 Tbsp. granulated onion
> ¼ cup water
> ¼ tsp. dry mustard

1. Blenderize all ingredients until smooth and creamy.
Yield: 2¼ cups

Tofu Mayonnaise

> 8 oz. firm-style tofu
> 1 Tbsp. water
> 2 Tbsp. lemon juice (freshly squeezed)
> 3 Tbsp. canola oil
> 1 tsp. Dijon-style mustard
> ½ tsp. sea salt

1. Combine all ingredients in a blender.
2. Purée until creamy smooth.
Yield: 1¼ cups

Tofu Mayonnaise (Oil-Free)

This can be used to spread on bread or to top steamed vegetables.

> 16 oz. firm-style tofu

1 Tbsp. apple-cider vinegar
1 Tbsp. lemon juice (freshly squeezed)
1 tsp. sea salt
3 Tbsp. water
½ tsp. Dijon-style mustard

1. Combine all ingredients in a blender and purée until creamy smooth.
2. Stop blender. Clear food from sides of blender and purée again.

Yield: 2 cups

Umeboshi Dressing

2 tsp. umeboshi paste
½ tsp. onion (minced)
½ tsp. toasted sesame oil
½ cup water

1. Purée the umeboshi paste and onion in a suribachi or blender.
2. Add sesame oil and water. Mix well.

Yield: ½ cup

Umeboshi Garlic Dressing

May be served over steamed vegetables or salad.

¼ cup umeboshi vinegar
⅓ cup extra-virgin olive oil
1 tsp. garlic (minced)
1 Tbsp. natural soy sauce

1. Combine all ingredients and use a whisk to blend.

Yield: ½ cup

Green Goddess Spread

This spread will keep in the refrigerator for three to four days. It can be served as a dip or spread with vegetables or bread. Delicious!

> 16 oz. firm-style tofu
> 2 cups spinach
> ¼ cup canola oil
> 2 Tbsp. apple-cider vinegar
> ½ tsp. Dijon-style mustard
> ½ tsp. sea salt
> ½ cup scallions (sliced)
> ½ cup parsley (chopped)

1. Blenderize the first 6 ingredients until creamy smooth, adding a little water if necessary to help blend.
2. Stir in scallions and parsley.
3. Taste and adjust seasonings.

Yield: 3 cups

Chickpea Spread

> 2 cups cooked chickpeas
> 1 cup onions (chopped and sautéed)
> ½ tsp. sea salt
> 2 Tbsp. raw sesame tahini
> 1 Tbsp. water, if needed

1. Place all ingredients in a blender.
2. Blend until smooth. Add a small amount of water if necessary to blend.

Yield: 3 cups

Lentil Spread

1 cup green lentils (washed and drained)
4 cups water
1 Tbsp. canola oil
3 cups onions (chopped)
½ tsp. sea salt
2 Tbsp. water

1. Place lentils and 4 cups water in a pot and bring to a boil.
2. Cover pot and reduce flame. Simmer 45 to 50 minutes.
3. Heat skillet and add oil.
4. Add onions and salt. Sauté until onions are transparent. Add 2 tablespoons water. Cover and simmer over very low flame until onions are very soft, about 20 minutes.
5. Place cooked lentils and onions in a blender and blend until smooth.
6. Transfer to a serving dish and allow to cool.

Yield: 4 cups

Millet "Butter"

Try this on Quick Corn Cakes, breads, or crackers.

1 tsp. kanten flakes
1½ cups water
1 cup hot, freshly cooked millet
¼ cup well-cooked carrots
¼ cup cashews
1 tsp. sea salt

1. Soften kanten flakes in water. Cook 3 minutes.
2. Blenderize all ingredients until smooth.
3. Pour into a bowl and chill several hours before serving.

Yield: 2⅔ cups

Dill Pickle and Miso Spread

I enjoy this spread on bread or rice cakes, or served as a condiment over rice.

> 8 oz. tofu (crumbled)
> 1/2 cup dill pickle (minced)
> 2 small carrots (grated)
> 1 onion (minced)
> 2 tsp. lemon juice (freshly squeezed)
> 2 Tbsp. brown-rice miso
> 1 Tbsp. canola oil

1. Combine the first 5 ingredients in a mixing bowl.
2. In separate bowl, combine miso and oil until smooth.
3. Stir miso mixture into tofu mixture.

Yield: 1¼ cups

Tofu Miso Spread

> 16 oz. firm-style tofu
> 2 Tbsp. miso
> 1/4 cup raw sesame tahini
> 4 Tbsp. parsley (minced)
> 3 Tbsp. scallions (sliced)
> 1 clove garlic (minced)

1. Preheat oven to 350 degrees.
2. Combine tofu, miso, and tahini in a mixing bowl. Stir in parsley, scallions, and garlic.
3. Press into an oiled 8-inch-square baking dish.
4. Bake uncovered at 350 degrees for 25 minutes.

Yield: 2½ cups

Desserts

One of the biggest misconceptions about natural-foods cooking, and especially about macrobiotics, is that there are no desserts. However, natural-foods and macrobiotic cooking provide all the sweet desserts you can eat, but do it without refined sugar, eggs, butter, or artificial flavors.

We have been conditioned to think that sugar is the only source of sweetness, but sweet taste is available from many different sources. Health-conscious people want sweet desserts, but they don't want the harmful effects of sugar. Sugar causes many health problems. One of the most common is hypoglycemia, or low blood sugar. People who suffer from low blood sugar have low energy. They often feel tired, nervous, anxious, and moody. They sleep poorly and get colds easily. They walk around with only half the energy and stamina they would have otherwise.

Sugar also robs the body of minerals, and minerals form the basis for a healthy immune system, as shown in the chapter, Meals That Heal, pages 199-205. Sugar is a fuel, which your cells need to do their jobs. But your cells also need many raw materials to perform: Bone cells need calcium, phosphorus, and protein; muscles need protein, calcium, phosphorus, and other minerals. Immune cells need zinc, selenium, magnesium, and vitamins A, B, C, and E. Usually, the refined foods that contain sugar are devoid of these essential nutrients. The sugar provides fuel, but not the essential nutrients for healthy metabolism (or proper cellular function). Consequently, the cells have to steal these nutrients from other sources in the body, such as bone and muscle, to adequately perform their tasks. In the end, sugar causes a net loss of nutrition within your body. It is essentially weakening.

People are growing more sophisticated about their diets and

about how food affects them. They know how they feel when they eat a refined dessert that contains sugar. They also know how they feel when they eat a food that contains whole-grain flour (with the vitamins and minerals present) and a natural sweetener.

Yet, everyone likes a sweet-tasting dessert; desserts make us feel good. We just don't want to get sick from them. So here are my recipes for the best of both worlds — sweet and healthy desserts.

Carob Cake

This cake can be frosted or simply served with Tofu "Whipped Cream."

> 1 cup water or soy milk
> 1/2 cup canola oil
> 1 tsp. vanilla
> 1 1/2 cups maple syrup
> 2 tsp. rice vinegar
> 3 1/2 cups whole-wheat pastry flour
> 1/2 cup carob powder
> 1 1/2 tsp. baking soda
> 1/4 tsp. sea salt

1. Preheat oven to 350 degrees. Oil 2, 8-inch-round pans.
2. Combine first 5 ingredients in mixing bowl and use a whisk to blend well.
3. Combine flour, carob, baking soda, and salt in a separate bowl and stir well.
4. Whisk dry ingredients into wet ingredients.
5. Pour batter into the oiled pans and bake at 350 degrees for approximately 45 minutes.

Yield: 2-layer cake

Carrot Cake

This is a delicious birthday cake when decorated with Tofu "Whipped Cream." Everybody likes it and it's easy to make.

> 2½ cups whole-wheat pastry flour
> ½ cup rice flour
> 1½ tsp. baking soda
> ¼ tsp. sea salt
> 1 tsp. cinnamon
> ¾ cup corn oil
> 1¼ cups maple syrup
> 1 cup orange juice
> 16 oz. firm-style tofu
> 1 tsp. pure vanilla extract
> 5 cups carrots (grated)
> 1½ cups walnuts (chopped)
> ¾ cup raisins
> 1 cup grated coconut, optional for added moistness

1. Preheat oven to 350 degrees. Oil 2, 9-inch-square cake pans.
2. Mix together first 5 ingredients.
3. Combine next 5 ingredients in a blender or food processor and process until smooth.
4. Stir wet mixture into dry ingredients.
5. Add remaining ingredients and stir to combine.
6. Pour batter into the oiled pans. Bake at 350 degrees 35 to 40 minutes, or until toothpick inserted in center comes out clean.
7. Let cool 10 minutes before removing from pans.

Yield: 2 cakes

Apricot Apple Pie

double recipe Rolled Pie Crust, page 185
6 cups Granny Smith apples (peeled and thinly sliced)
1 Tbsp. maple syrup
1 Tbsp. apple juice
2 Tbsp. unbleached flour
8- to 10-oz. jar natural apricot jam

1. Preheat oven to 375 degrees. Oil a 9-inch pie plate.
2. Fit bottom crust into the oiled pie plate.
3. In a saucepan, combine apples with maple syrup and apple juice. Cook gently 5 minutes until apples are wilted. Remove from heat.
4. Stir in flour. Add apricot jam.
5. Place apple filling in bottom crust. Place top crust over pie. Seal edges and cut slits in top.
6. Bake at 375 degrees for 10 minutes. Reduce heat to 350 degrees and bake 30 minutes longer.

Yield: 1 pie

Fresh Cherry Pie

double recipe Rolled Pie Crust, page 185
¾ cup maple syrup
2 Tbsp. corn oil
¼ tsp. almond extract
3 Tbsp. unbleached flour
6 cups fresh cherries (pitted)

1. Preheat oven to 400 degrees. Oil a 9-inch pie plate.
2. Fit bottom crust into the oiled pie plate.
3. Combine maple syrup, oil, almond extract, and flour in mixing bowl. Toss in cherries and coat well.

4. Place cherry mixture in pie crust.
5. Roll out and cut top crust in 1/2-inch wide strips. Weave a lattice top over pie.
6. Bake at 400 degrees for 15 minutes. Reduce heat to 350 degrees and bake 25 minutes longer.
7. Let cool before cutting.

Yield: 1 pie

Cherry Pie

double recipe Rolled Pie Crust, page 185
16 oz. frozen pitted cherries
3/4 cup maple syrup
2 Tbsp. corn oil
1/4 tsp. almond extract
1/3 cup unbleached flour

1. Preheat oven to 375 degrees. Oil a 9-inch pie plate.
2. Fit bottom crust into the oiled pie plate.
3. Remove frozen cherries from package and place in a saucepan. Heat cherries over medium flame until liquid is released and they begin to simmer.
4. In a mixing bowl, use a wire whisk to combine syrup, oil, almond extract, and flour.
5. Combine syrup mixture with cherries and stir until heated through.
6. Pour cherry mixture into pie crust.
7. Place top crust over pie. Seal edges of the crust by pressing with tines of a fork. Cut slits in top crust.
8. Bake at 375 degrees 35 to 40 minutes until browned on top and bubbling.

Yield: 1 pie

Strawberry Pear Pie

An old American favorite with an Oriental twist.

> **2 Tbsp. kanten flakes**
> **2 cups pear juice**
> **1 Tbsp. pure vanilla extract**
> **¼ cup maple syrup, or ⅓ cup rice syrup**
> **10 oz firm-style tofu**
> **Rolled Pie Crust, page 185 (baked)**
> **10 fresh strawberries**

1. Dissolve kanten flakes in juice. Bring to a boil and simmer 3 minutes.
2. Transfer to a blender and add vanilla, maple syrup, and tofu. Blend until creamy smooth.
3. Pour into baked pie crust. Garnish with fresh strawberries.
4. Chill overnight before serving.

Yield: 1 pie

Cranberry Pecan Pie

> **3½ cups cranberries**
> **½ cup raisins**
> **⅓ cup pecans**
> **¼ cup unbleached flour**
> **1 tsp. arrowroot**
> **½ tsp. cinnamon**
> **1 cup maple syrup**
> **¼ cup orange juice**
> **3 Tbsp. oil**
> **9-inch pie shell (frozen or homemade)**
> **Tofu "Whipped Cream," page 196, as topping**

1. Preheat oven to 400 degrees.

2. Chop cranberries briefly in food processor.
3. Transfer cranberries to a large mixing bowl. Add raisins, pecans, flour, arrowroot, and cinnamon.
4. In a small mixing bowl, use a whisk to combine the maple syrup, orange juice, and oil.
5. Stir liquid ingredients into dry ingredients.
6. Spoon filling into the pie shell. Bake 45 minutes at 400 degrees.
7. Let cool before slicing. Serve with a dollop of tofu "whipped cream."

Yield: 1 pie

Cranberry Apple Pie

5 cups apples (thinly sliced)
1 cup cranberries
³/₄ cup maple syrup
2 Tbsp. corn oil
4 Tbsp. unbleached flour
9-inch pie shell (unbaked)
¹/₃ recipe Granola Crumb Crust, page 184, as topping

1. Preheat oven to 400 degrees.
2. Combine apples and cranberries and place in pie shell.
3. Combine maple syrup, oil, and flour in a mixing bowl.
4. Drizzle the syrup mixture over the fruit. Sprinkle granola topping on top.
5. Bake 15 minutes at 400 degrees.
6. Reduce heat to 350 degrees and bake 35 minutes longer. Let cool before slicing.

Yield: 1 pie

Tofu "Cheesecake"

A wonderful summer dessert garnished with sliced fresh straw-berries, Peach Topping, or Apple Topping. The secret to making this "cheesecake" is blending the ingredients until smooth and creamy.

    16 oz. firm-style tofu
    2 heaping Tbsp. raw sesame tahini
    3/4 cup maple syrup
    2 Tbsp. lemon juice (freshly squeezed)
    1/4 tsp. sea salt
    2 tsp. pure vanilla extract
    Rolled Pie Crust, page 185 (baked)

1. Preheat oven to 350 degrees.
2. Blend the first 6 ingredients until smooth.
3. Pour into baked pie crust and bake at 350 degrees for approx-imately 35 minutes.
4. Chill until set before slicing.

Yield: 1 pie

Carob Swirl Pie

    16 oz. firm-style tofu
    1/3 cup canola oil
    3/4 cup maple syrup
    2 tsp. kuzu or arrowroot
    2 tsp. pure vanilla extract
    1 Tbsp. carob powder
    1 tsp. grain coffee
    1 pinch sea salt
    1/4 cup carob chips
    Granola Crumb Crust, page 184 (baked)

1. Preheat oven to 350 degrees.

2. Combine first 8 ingredients in blender and mix well.
3. Melt carob chips in a double boiler over boiling water.
4. Using a spoon or table knife, swirl half the melted carob chips into the tofu mixture. Pour tofu mixture into the baked crumb crust.
5. Swirl remaining melted carob chips over top of pie.
6. Bake at 350 degrees for 30 minutes or until filling no longer sticks to fingers when touched. Cool before slicing.

Yield: 1 pie

Millet Blueberry Pie

> 3 cups apple juice
> 3 cups pineapple juice
> 1 cup millet (washed and drained)
> ½ cup maple syrup or other liquid sweetener
> 2 cups blueberries (fresh or frozen)
> 4 Tbsp. plus 1 tsp. kanten flakes
> 1 Tbsp. pure vanilla extract
> ¼ tsp. sea salt
> 2 Rolled Pie Crusts, page 185
> 2 Tbsp. natural apricot jam
> 1 tsp. lemon rind (grated)

1. Place first 8 ingredients in saucepan and bring to a boil. Cover and simmer 30 minutes.
2. While filling is simmering, preheat oven to 350 degrees. Prepare and bake pie crusts 15 minutes.
3. Stir the apricot jam and lemon rind into the filling. Let cool 30 minutes.
4. Pour half the mixture at a time into blender or food processor. Blend at high speed until creamy smooth.
5. Pour into cooled pie crusts. Chill overnight before serving.

Yield: 2 pies

Creamy Lemon Pie

Very easy, even for the novice, and a big hit with every sweet tooth. For a milder taste, substitute apple juice for pineapple juice.

$\frac{2}{3}$ cup cashews
3 cups pineapple juice
$\frac{1}{8}$ tsp. sea salt
$\frac{1}{4}$ cup plus 2 Tbsp. maple syrup
4 Tbsp. kuzu
1 Tbsp. lemon juice
1 tsp. lemon rind (grated)
Granola Crumb Crust, page 184 (baked)

1. Blend first 6 ingredients until creamy smooth.
2. Transfer to a saucepan and simmer until thick.
3. Turn flame off and stir in lemon rind.
4. Pour into baked crumb crust and chill overnight before serving.

Yield: 1 pie

Lemon Apricot Pie

2 cups water
$\frac{1}{2}$ cup cream-of-wheat
8 oz. firm-style tofu
$\frac{3}{4}$ cup maple syrup
1 tsp. lemon rind (grated)
2 Tbsp. lemon juice (freshly squeezed)
$\frac{1}{4}$ tsp. almond extract
1 pinch sea salt
10 oz. natural apricot jam
1 cup walnuts (roasted and chopped)

1. Bring water to a boil and add cream-of-wheat, stirring with

wire whisk.

2. Reduce heat and simmer 3 minutes.
3. Combine remaining ingredients, except walnuts, in a food processor and purée until smooth.
4. Add the tofu mixture to the cream-of-wheat. Simmer and stir until heated through.
5. Sprinkle the walnuts in an oiled 9-inch pie plate.
6. Pour the tofu mixture over the walnuts.
7. When the pie is completely cool, invert it over a plate and cut into 8 equal slices.

Yield: 1 pie

Lemon Tofu "Cheesecake"

This "cheesecake" was a big hit in a recent holiday cooking class.

> 10 oz. firm-style tofu
> ¾ cup pineapple juice
> ¼ tsp. sea salt
> 2 Tbsp. arrowroot
> ¾ cup maple syrup
> ½ cup cashews (finely ground)
> 1 Tbsp. pure vanilla extract
> ½ tsp. lemon extract
> ⅛ tsp. almond extract
> Granola Crumb Crust, page 184 (baked)

1. Preheat oven to 350 degrees.
2. Crumble tofu into a mixing bowl. Add remaining ingredients.
3. In blender, blend in 2 batches until creamy smooth.
4. Pour into baked crumb crust. Bake 25 minutes at 350 degrees.
5. Chill overnight before serving.

Yield: 1 pie

Raspberry Pie

double recipe Rolled Pie Crust, page 185
3 Tbsp. apple juice
⅓ cup maple syrup
3 Tbsp. unbleached flour
20 oz. frozen raspberries (thawed and drained)

1. Preheat oven to 400 degrees. Oil a 9-inch pie plate.
2. Fit bottom crust into the oiled pie plate.
3. Using a whisk, combine juice, maple syrup, and flour. Mix with raspberries.
4. Spoon filling into bottom crust.
5. Cover with top crust. Seal edges and cut slits in top.
6. Bake 35 to 40 minutes at 400 degrees.

Yield: 1 pie

Sesame Squash Pie

Rolled Pie Crust, page 185
2½ cups baked winter squash
¾ cup maple syrup
1 tsp. cinnamon
½ tsp. nutmeg
2 Tbsp. raw sesame tahini
1 pinch sea salt
4 Tbsp. kuzu
½ cup soy milk

1. Preheat oven to 350 degrees. Oil a 9-inch pie plate.
2. Fit crust into the oiled pie plate. Bake 12 minutes at 350 degrees. Let cool.
3. Increase oven heat to 375 degrees.
4. Blenderize remaining ingredients until creamy smooth.

5. Stop blender and use a rubber spatula to clear food from sides of container. Purée again.
6. Pour into crust and bake 10 minutes at 375 degrees. Reduce oven to 350 and bake 20 minutes longer, or until set.
7. Let cool before slicing.
Yield: 1 pie

Squash Pie

Bake squash early in the day and allow it to cool and firm up before using in this recipe. Freshly baked, warm squash will not give best results.

> **Pressed Pie Crust, page 184**
> **2½ cups baked butternut squash**
> **10 oz. firm-style tofu**
> **1 cup maple syrup**
> **2 tsp. pure vanilla extract**
> **2 heaping Tbsp. almond butter**
> **2 tsp. cinnamon**
> **1 pinch sea salt**

1. Preheat oven to 350 degrees. Oil a 9-inch pie plate.
2. Press crust into the oiled pie plate. Bake 10 minutes at 350 degrees.
3. Blenderize all remaining ingredients until creamy smooth.
4. Stop blender and use a rubber spatula to clear food from sides of container. Purée again.
5. Pour into pie crust and bake 30 minutes at 350 degrees.
6. Allow to cool before slicing.
Yield: 1 pie

Pressed Pie Crust

For those of us who dislike rolling out pie crusts, this one is quick and easy. Just combine ingredients and press into a pie plate.

1 cup whole-wheat pastry flour
1 cup oat flakes
1 pinch sea salt
⅓ cup canola oil
3 Tbsp. water or apple juice

1. Preheat oven to 350 degrees. Oil a 9-inch pie plate.
2. Combine first 3 ingredients in a small mixing bowl.
3. Work the oil into the flour mixture, using a fork or wooden spoon.
4. Sprinkle water over the mixture and press into the oiled pie plate.
5. To bake crust completely, bake 10 minutes at 350 degrees and let cool before filling. (For pies that will be baked after they are filled, follow baking directions in the pie recipe.)

Yield: 1 crust

Granola Crumb Crust

3 cups granola (ground in blender)
5 Tbsp. apple juice
2 Tbsp. corn oil

1. Preheat oven to 350 degrees.
2. Place ground granola in a mixing bowl.
3. In a separate bowl combine apple juice and oil.
4. Stir apple-juice mixture into granola and combine very well.
5. Press into a 9-inch pie plate.

6. Bake 20 minutes at 350 degrees.

7. Let cool completely before filling.

Yield: 1 crust

Rolled Pie Crust

Double this recipe to make a pie with a top crust.

> **1½ cups whole-wheat pastry flour**
> **1 pinch sea salt**
> **⅓ cup corn oil**
> **4 to 6 Tbsp. ice water**

1. Preheat oven to 350 degrees. Oil a 9-inch pie plate.
2. Combine flour and salt in a mixing bowl.
3. Combine oil and water in a separate bowl.
4. Stir the wet ingredients into dry. Gather the dough into a ball.
5. Lay a large piece of waxed paper on dampened work surface.
6. Place the pie dough on the waxed paper and cover with another sheet of waxed paper.
7. Roll the dough evenly from the center with a rolling pin.
8. Fit the dough into the oiled pie plate.
9. To bake crust completely, bake 10 to 15 minutes at 350 degrees and let cool before filling. (For pies that will be baked after they are filled, follow baking directions in the pie recipe.)

Yield: 1 crust

Oatmeal Raisin Cookies

3 cups oat flakes
1¹/₂ cups whole-wheat pastry flour
¹/₂ tsp. cinnamon
¹/₂ tsp. sea salt
1 cup rice syrup
3 Tbsp. corn oil
1 cup water
¹/₂ cup raisins
1 cup walnuts (roasted and chopped)

1. Combine oat flakes, flour, cinnamon, and salt.
2. In a small mixing bowl, whisk syrup, oil, and water.
3. Add wet ingredients to dry ingredients.
4. Fold in raisins and walnuts.
5. Set aside for 20 minutes to thicken.
6. Preheat oven to 350 degrees. Oil a cookie sheet.
7. Roll cookie dough into 2-inch balls and place on the oiled cookie sheet. Flatten slightly.
8. Bake at 350 degrees for 20 to 25 minutes.
Yield: 12 to 16 cookies

Oatmeal Cookies

2 cups oat flakes
1¹/₂ cups whole-wheat pastry flour
1¹/₂ tsp. aluminum-free baking powder
1 tsp. cinnamon
¹/₈ tsp. sea salt
¹/₂ cup corn oil
¹/₂ cup water
¹/₂ cup maple syrup

1 tsp. pure vanilla extract
½ cup walnuts (chopped)
¾ cup raisins

1. Preheat oven to 375 degrees. Oil a cookie sheet.
2. Combine oat flakes, flour, baking powder, cinnamon, and salt in a mixing bowl.
3. Combine oil, water, syrup, and vanilla in a smaller bowl.
4. Pour the wet ingredients into the dry ingredients and combine well.
5. Fold in the walnuts and raisins.
6. Use an ice-cream scoop to place mounds of cookie dough about 2 inches apart on the oiled cookie sheet. Slightly flatten each mound with moistened fingers.
7. Bake about 20 minutes at 375 degrees.

Yield: 10 to 12 cookies

Almond Cookies

¾ cup corn oil
½ cup maple syrup
2 cups whole-wheat pastry flour
¼ cup brown-rice flour
¾ cup almonds (ground)
1 tsp. arrowroot

1. Preheat oven to 350 degrees. Oil a cookie sheet.
2. Combine oil and syrup in a mixing bowl.
3. In a separate bowl, combine remaining ingredients.
4. Stir wet mixture into dry ingredients.
5. Roll into 2-inch balls and arrange on the oiled cookie sheet. Flatten slightly.
6. Bake at 350 degrees about 10 minutes.

Yield: 12 to 14 cookies

Wheat-Free Almond Cookies

1 cup maple syrup
2/3 cup corn oil
1/2 cup almonds (ground)
4 cups brown-rice flour
1/2 tsp. sea salt
2 tsp. cinnamon
1 tsp. dry ginger

1. Preheat oven to 350 degrees. Oil a cookie sheet.
2. Blend syrup and oil until creamy. Add ground almonds.
3. Combine flour with salt, cinnamon, and ginger. Fold into syrup mixture.
4. Roll into 2-inch balls and place on the oiled cookie sheet. Flatten slightly.
5. Bake at 350 degrees about 20 minutes or until edges are lightly browned.

Yield: 24 cookies

Granola Cookies

4 cups oat flakes
1 Tbsp. aluminum-free baking powder
1 Tbsp. arrowroot
1¾ cups whole-wheat pastry flour
1 cup shredded coconut
1 cup sunflower seeds (lightly toasted)
1/2 cup sesame seeds (lightly toasted)
16 oz. firm-style tofu
2 cups maple syrup
1 cup corn oil

1. Combine the first 7 ingredients in a large mixing bowl.
2. Purée tofu, syrup, and oil in a food processor.

3. Stir wet ingredients into dry ingredients.
4. Set aside for 20 minutes to thicken.
5. Preheat oven to 350 degrees. Oil a 12x18-inch cookie sheet.
6. Place mounds of cookie dough about 1 inch apart on the cookie sheet using an ice-cream scoop. Flatten slightly with moistened fingers.
7. Bake 20 to 25 minutes at 350 degrees.
Yield: 24 cookies

Holiday Carrot Cookies

$\frac{1}{2}$ cup canola oil
$\frac{3}{4}$ cup maple syrup
1 tsp. pure vanilla extract
1 cup whole-wheat pastry flour
$\frac{1}{2}$ cup brown-rice flour
$\frac{3}{4}$ cup oat flakes
$\frac{1}{4}$ tsp. sea salt
$1\frac{1}{4}$ tsp. aluminum-free baking powder
$\frac{1}{4}$ tsp. cinnamon
1 cup carrots (grated)
$\frac{3}{4}$ cup raisins
1 cup walnuts (chopped)
$\frac{1}{2}$ cup dates (chopped)

1. Preheat oven to 350 degrees. Oil a cookie sheet.
2. Whisk together oil, maple syrup, and vanilla.
3. Combine flour, oats, salt, baking powder, and cinnamon in a separate bowl.
4. Stir wet ingredients into dry ingredients.
5. Gently fold in carrots, raisins, walnuts, and dates.
6. Use an ice-cream scoop to place mounds of cookie dough onto the oiled cookie sheet. Flatten slightly.
7. Bake 25 to 30 minutes at 350 degrees.
Yield: 12 to 14 cookies

Carrot Walnut Cookies

> 2 cups whole-wheat pastry flour
> 1 cup brown-rice flour
> 1 pinch sea salt
> ½ cup date sugar
> 4 oz. tofu
> 2 cups maple syrup
> 2 tsp. pure vanilla extract
> 1 cup carrots (grated)
> 1¼ cups walnuts (chopped)
> ½ cup coconut flakes, optional

1. Preheat oven to 350 degrees. Oil a cookie sheet.
2. Combine flour, salt, and sugar in a mixing bowl.
3. Blenderize tofu, syrup, and vanilla until smooth.
4. Add tofu mixture to dry ingredients and mix well.
5. Stir in carrots, walnuts, and coconut.
6. Use an ice-cream scoop to place mounds of cookie dough onto the oiled cookie sheet. Flatten slightly.
7. Bake at 350 degrees about 25 minutes.

Yield: 20 cookies

Oat Walnut Cookies

> 1½ cups oat flakes
> 1 cup whole-wheat pastry flour
> ½ tsp. aluminum-free baking powder
> ¼ tsp. sea salt
> ½ cup corn oil
> ⅓ cup maple syrup
> ½ tsp. pure vanilla extract
> ¾ cup walnuts (roasted and chopped)

1. Preheat oven to 350 degrees. Oil a cookie sheet.

2. Grind oat flakes in a food processor and transfer to a mixing bowl.
3. Add flour, baking powder, and salt to oats.
4. Combine oil, syrup, and vanilla. Stir into oat mixture.
5. Fold in walnuts.
6. With moistened hands, shape into 20 small balls and place on the oiled cookie sheet. Flatten slightly.
7. Bake 12 minutes at 350 degrees.

Yield: 20 cookies

Walnut Cookies

¾ cup corn oil
¾ cup maple syrup
1 tsp. pure vanilla extract
1½ cups whole-wheat pastry flour
1 cup brown-rice flour
1 cup unbleached flour
1 pinch sea salt
1 tsp. cinnamon
1 tsp. arrowroot
1½ cups walnuts (chopped)
½ cup raisins

1. Preheat oven to 350 degrees. Oil a cookie sheet.
2. Combine oil, syrup, and vanilla in small mixing bowl. Beat with a whisk until thickened.
3. In a separate bowl, combine remaining ingredients except walnuts and raisins.
4. Add liquid ingredients to dry ingredients and stir gently.
5. Stir in walnuts and raisins.
6. Roll into 2-inch balls and place the oiled cookie sheet. Flatten centers slightly with moistened fingers.
7. Bake at 350 degrees 17 minutes.

Yield: 14 cookies

Date Bars

These bars are really for special occasions. I usually make them once a year, during holidays.

Filling
2 cups pitted dates
½ cup toasted garbanzo flour
1 cup grated coconut
1 tsp. cinnamon
½ cup maple syrup

Topping
2 cups oat flakes
¼ tsp. sea salt
½ tsp. cinnamon
½ cup corn oil
3 Tbsp. maple syrup
½ cup whole-wheat pastry flour

1. Preheat oven to 350 degrees. Oil a 9-inch-square baking pan.
2. Combine filling ingredients in a blender and blend until smooth.
3. Transfer to the oiled baking pan.
4. Combine topping ingredients in a mixing bowl.
5. Sprinkle topping evenly over filling.
6. Bake uncovered 25 minutes at 350 degrees.
7. Let cool and cut into bars.
Yield: 12 bars

Amasake Pudding

8 oz. amasake (prepared)
1 Tbsp. rice syrup
½ tsp. ginger juice (squeezed from grated fresh ginger root)

1 tsp. kuzu, dissolved in 2 tsp. water
almond slices (roasted), for garnish

1. Place amasake in a saucepan over low heat.
2. Add syrup and ginger juice. Bring to a slow simmer.
3. Whisk in the kuzu and simmer until slightly thickened.
4. Pour into serving dishes and garnish with almond slices.
Yield: 1 cup

Blueberry Crisp

4 cups blueberries
1 cup apple juice
1 Tbsp. maple syrup
2 Tbsp. kuzu, dissolved in 2 Tbsp. water
2 cups oat flakes
1/2 cup whole-wheat pastry flour
1/4 tsp. sea salt
1/2 tsp. cinnamon
1/2 cup corn oil
3 Tbsp. maple syrup

1. Place blueberries, juice, and syrup in saucepan and bring to a simmer.
2. Whisk in the dissolved kuzu and stir until thickened, about 2 minutes. Remove from heat.
3. Preheat oven to 350 degrees. Oil a 9-inch-square baking pan.
4. Combine oats, flour, salt, and cinnamon in a mixing bowl.
5. Combine oil and maple syrup in a separate bowl. Stir into the oat mixture to make oat topping.
6. Place blueberry filling in the oiled baking pan.
7. Sprinkle oat topping evenly over the filling.
8. Bake uncovered 30 minutes at 350 degrees.
Servings: 9

Apple Brown Betty

> 6 cups apples (sliced)
> 1 cup oat flakes
> 1/3 cup walnuts (ground)
> 1/4 cup brown-rice flour
> 1 tsp. cinnamon
> 1/2 cup raisins
> 1/4 cup apple juice
> 1 Tbsp. maple syrup

1. Preheat oven to 350 degrees. Oil a 9-inch pie plate.
2. Place the apples in the pie plate.
3. Combine remaining ingredients in a separate bowl and sprinkle over the apples.
4. Bake uncovered at 350 degrees for 25 to 30 minutes.

Servings: 9

Peach Kanten

Refreshing dessert in Tokyo and Texas.

> 4 cups apple juice
> 2 tsp. maple syrup or rice syrup
> 1/3 cup kanten flakes, packed in measuring cup
> 2 cups peaches, fresh or frozen (thawed)
> 1 heaping tsp. kuzu, dissolved in 1 Tbsp. water
> 1 tsp. pure vanilla extract
> Tofu "Whipped Cream," page 196

1. Combine juice, syrup, and kanten flakes in a saucepan. Bring to a boil.
2. Add peaches and simmer 1 minute.
3. Stir in the kuzu mixture and vanilla extract.
4. Pour the mixture into an 8-inch-square dish and chill until set.

5. Cut into squares and serve with a dollop of tofu "whipped cream."

Servings: 9

Apple Topping

Delicious with Tofu "Cheesecake;" arrange apple slices over the top of the "cheesecake" and chill several hours before slicing.

> **3 apples (thinly sliced)**
> **1 tsp. cinnamon**
> **2 Tbsp. maple syrup**

1. Sauté apple slices in oiled skillet until slightly wilted.
2. Sprinkle with cinnamon and maple syrup.
3. Cover skillet and turn off flame. Leave covered for 1 or 2 minutes.

Yield: 1$^1/_2$ cups

Peach Topping

Delicious with Tofu "Cheesecake;" pour hot topping over "cheesecake" and chill before serving.

> **1 cup peaches, fresh or frozen (thawed)**
> **3 Tbsp. maple syrup**
> **1 Tbsp. lemon juice (freshly squeezed)**
> **2 Tbsp. kuzu, dissolved in 4 Tbsp. apple juice**

1. Blend all ingredients in blender.
2. Pour into saucepan and bring to a boil. Simmer just until thick.

Yield: 1 cup

Strawberry Tofu Frosting

Delicious as a topping for fruit crisp or spread over cake.

> **16 oz. firm-style tofu**
> **1 cup natural strawberry jam**
> **1 tsp. lemon juice (freshly squeezed)**
> **1 Tbsp. maple syrup**

1. Place all ingredients in a blender and purée until smooth.
Yield: 2½ cups approx.

Tofu "Whipped Cream"

Serve this topping over fruit crisp or Carrot Cake for an elegant dessert.

> **16 oz. firm-style tofu**
> **5 Tbsp. maple syrup**
> **¼ cup water**
> **2 Tbsp. almond butter**
> **1 tsp. pure vanilla extract**
> **1 pinch sea salt**

1. Blend tofu, syrup, and water in blender until smooth.
2. Add remaining ingredients and continue blending until creamy, adding an additional 1 to 2 tablespoons water if needed for desired consistency.
Yield: 2 cups

Cashew "Whipped Cream"

½ cup cashews (ground)
½ cup water
2 Tbsp. maple syrup
¼ tsp. pure vanilla extract
1 pinch sea salt

1. Process all ingredients in a blender until smooth.
Yield: ¾ cup

Carob Tahini "Fudge"

A rich, fudge-like treat without the chocolate.

½ cup water
4 Tbsp. kanten flakes
½ cup maple syrup
1½ Tbsp. kuzu
½ cup carob flour
½ cup raw sesame tahini
1 Tbsp. pure vanilla extract
½ cup walnuts (chopped)

1. Place water in a saucepan and stir in kanten flakes. Bring to a boil.
2. Lower flame and simmer 2 to 3 minutes.
3. Place maple syrup, kuzu, carob flour, and tahini in a blender. Blend until smooth.
4. Add blended mixture to saucepan and bring back to a boil. Lower flame and simmer 2 to 3 minutes, stirring constantly.
5. Remove from heat. Stir in vanilla and walnuts.
6. Pour into an 8-inch-square dish and let cool before slicing into squares.
Yield: 9 squares

══Meals that Heal══

Perhaps, like me, you became interested in diet and health because of some personal health concern, or a concern for the health of a loved one. If either of these is the case, you're probably wondering how the macrobiotic diet can help improve health. "What part does diet play in the healing process?" is the question many people are asking today.

Food was the original medicine of human beings. All traditional health systems of both East and West used plant foods as their way of treating disease. Whether the medical system was Chinese, Greek, Ayurvedic, or native American, that system depended upon the power of plant foods to overcome disease. Food has been the basis of health care for tens of thousands of years.

Indeed, people have depended upon a certain type of diet for maintaining health and vitality throughout human evolution. Composed chiefly of whole grains, beans, vegetables, fruit, and small quantities of animal foods, that diet shaped the very structure of our bodies. We have a long digestive tract, typical of herbivores. We have thirty-two teeth, twenty of which are molars, ideal for grinding grains and vegetables.

Also, we developed an intolerance for excess fat and cholesterol. Too much of either is poisonous and even lethal. We also have distinct limits on the amount of protein we can consume without getting sick. When our protein consumption exceeds 15 to 20 percent of our total calories, we develop such illnesses as gout, a form of arthritis. Scientists are now demonstrating that a diet rich in animal protein leads to a wide variety of cancers.

We have other dietary pecularities. For example, we developed the need for abundant fiber for healthy digestion and elimination; we need a wide array of vitamins and minerals, typical of unrefined foods; and we have an overwhelming need for complex carbohydrates as our principle source of energy. No other food provides us with so healthy and efficient a source of energy as complex carbohydrates, from grains, vegetables, and fruit. Finally, we need a certain amount of clean water.

We developed distinct nutritional needs and limitations. The liver and kidneys can cleanse only so many toxins from the blood; the intestines can eliminate only so much waste. When these and other limitations are exceeded, the poisons we consume begin to accumulate in our blood, our organs, and cells. Eventually, they cause disease.

Atherosclerosis, which is cholesterol plaque that clogs arteries throughout the body, is a form of accumulation that prevents blood and oxygen from flowing to cells, tissues, and organs. Once cells are deprived of oxygen, they either suffocate and die, or they may mutate. The DNA, or genetic brain within the cell, can instruct the cell to multiply in ways that are harmful to the body, and thus cancer develops.

The amount of poison the average person consumes is mind-boggling. Cholesterol, pesticides, herbicides, artificial colors and flavors, heavy metals, radioactive particles, PCPs, a wide variety of drugs, viruses, and bacteria — the list is endless. When we consume these poisons, while eating fat and cholesterol that deprive organs of oxygen, the combined effect is overwhelming. For the immune system, it's like trying to fight a war while being suffocated.

Miraculously the human body battles all of this to maintain life, and in most cases it survives for many decades. Our ability to neutralize and eliminate poisons is a miracle to behold. But what would life be like if so much of our energy weren't directed toward the mammoth job of fighting poisons? How much easier would it be to reach our human potential in life? Can we even know our potential in the face of so many poisons that drain us of life energy?

But when the pollution level reaches a certain point, the

body's internal chemistry becomes so toxic that illness is inevitable. Not only do the myriad poisons overwhelm the immune system, but some of these poisons act directly upon immune cells to make them ineffective.

Saturated fat has been shown to adversely affect the cell membranes of the macrophage and phagocyte cells, the large scavenger cells that patrol the blood stream looking for foreign objects and pathogens that invade the body. The fat coats the membranes of these cells, causing them to lose their sensitivity and their ability to determine self from not-self. Without this ability, these cells allow the bacteria, virus, or cancer cells to multiply, and eventually take over the system.

Also, once inside the system, dietary fat oxidizes, or becomes rancid. As these oxidized fats decay, they cause atoms to lose electrons and form free radicals, which are highly charged molecules that are extremely reactive and destructive to cells and DNA. Once an atom loses one or more electrons, it begins to steal electrons from neighboring atoms. These neighboring atoms, in turn, steal electrons from other atoms, causing chain reactions that destabilize molecules and whole tissues. As molecules and cells break down, mutations are formed, causing many other serious illnesses.

Dr. Joe M. McCord, a biochemist at the University of Southern Alabama College of Medicine told the *New York Times* that "the further along we get, the more we are overwhelmed by the number of disease states that involve free radicals." Scientists at the University of Southern Alabama and the University of California at Davis maintain that free radicals are involved in the onset of as many as sixty diseases, including cancer, Alzheimer's disease, Parkinson's disease, cataracts, arthritis, and immune disorders.

However, just as certain foods initiate the free-radical process, other foods reverse it. Certain vegetables contain nutrients called antioxidants, or free-radical scavengers. These foods donate electrons to imbalanced atoms and restore harmony to molecules, cells, and tissues. These foods stop the decay process that leads to illness. Among the most effective antioxidants are beta-carotene (found in squash, carrots, broccoli, and collard greens), and vitamins C and E. Vitamin C is found in abundance in fruits and vegetables; vitamin E in whole grains and seeds.

Studies have shown that the strength of the immune system is dependent upon the presence of certain nutrients that are common in whole grains, vegetables, and sea vegetables. These nutrients include zinc, selenium, beta-carotene, manganese, magnesium, copper, calcium, iron, and vitamins C and E.

It is only in this century that we stopped using diet as a means of treating disease. Now, after decades of dependence upon pharmaceuticals and surgery, we are returning to the healing power of food and traditional methods of healing for answers to our most widespread killer diseases such as heart disease, diabetes, cancer, and now immune-deficiency diseases.

The change began in 1977 when the Senate Select Committee on Nutrition and Human Needs studied the relationship between diet and health and found that six of the ten leading causes of death were directly related to the modern diet. Since the mid-1970s, we have heard that message repeated again and again.

The United States Surgeon General and other health authorities now urge us to change our way of eating from a diet based largely on animal foods such as red meat, dairy products, and eggs to one based on whole grains and fresh vegetables.

In April of 1992, the United States Department of Agriculture made that advice official. The USDA scrapped the old "Four Food Groups" and replaced it with a pyramid design that recommended we make whole grains our principle food. This is the diet science recommends as a way of maintaining and improving health. These guidelines demonstrate that we are moving more toward the diet humans evolved on, and the diet that most humans still consume.

In 1990, Cornell University scientists reported the results of a long-term study in which the diets and disease patterns of sixty-five hundred Chinese were examined. The study revealed that the Chinese diet, which consists largely of whole grains, vegetables, and very small amounts of animal foods, protects against virtually all the common degenerative diseases, including heart disease, cancer, osteoporosis, diabetes, and high blood pressure.

Chinese cancer rates are low. Breast and reproductive cancers are rare in China. The Chinese obtain only 7 percent of their protein from animal foods; Americans get more than 70 percent of their protein from animal sources. Excess animal protein has been linked to cancer and osteoporosis.

Most Chinese do not consume dairy products, yet osteoporosis also is rare in China. Interestingly, the Chinese consume only half the calcium Americans do. They get their calcium almost exclusively from plant foods such as leafy green vegetables and sea vegetables.

The Chinese eat 20 percent more calories than Americans do, but obesity is rare among Chinese. The reason for the difference: Chinese eat only a third as much fat as Americans and twice the complex carbohydrates from grains and vegetables. Complex carbohydrate foods are easily burned as fuel or consumed by the body to produce heat. In other words, they are not readily converted into fat.

The Chinese blood cholesterol levels are also uniformly low. They range from 88 mg/dl to 165 mg/dl, nearly half of what Americans average, which is from 155 mg/dl to 274 mg/dl. Blood cholesterol is a good indicator of illness. There are some regional dietary differences in China: In places where a higher fat and cholesterol diet is consumed, the disease rates are also higher. We think of blood cholesterol as related only to heart disease, but in fact cholesterol level is related to all degenerative illnesses, because high cholesterol prevents oxygen from going to cells.

"So far we've seen that plasma cholesterol is a good predictor of the kinds of diseases people are going to get," said Dr. T. Colin Campbell, biochemist at Cornell and organizer of the Chinese study. "Those with higher cholesterol levels are prone to the diseases of affluence—cancer, heart disease, and diabetes," said Dr. Campbell. After reviewing the evidence, Dr. Campbell summarized his thoughts this way: "We're basically a vegetarian species and should be eating a wide variety of plant foods and minimizing our intake of animal foods."

The wisdom of the past is returning to the present. We're finding that some of the ways of our ancestors may be helpful to our own times. In fact, there is much to learn from the traditional methods, especially their ways of promoting health and treating illness. Simply stated: A natural whole-foods diet can help strengthen our physical health and vitality and can help protect us from degenerative disease.

Still, I do not want to give you the impression that we all have to start eating an Asian diet. In fact, all traditional peoples used whole grains, vegetables, beans, fruit, fermented foods, and condiments in their own creative ways. Many people, including the Irish, the French, the American Indian, and the Asian ate sea vegetables too.

The diet our bodies have evolved on, the diet that supports our health best, looks like this: whole grains such as brown rice, barley, whole wheat, millet, oats, corn, and buckwheat; vegetables, including leafy greens, roots, and tubers; beans such as azuki, black beans, chickpeas, lentils, limas, mung beans, navy beans, peas, soybeans, split peas, and tofu; sea vegetables such as arame, dulse, hijiki, nori, wakame, and kombu; fermented foods such as miso, natural soy sauce, sauerkraut, tempeh, natto, pickles, umeboshi plums, vinegars, and other traditionally processed foods; and small amounts of fruit, nuts, seeds, and animal foods, especially fish.

There are many ideas about what health is and a lot of advice about how to achieve it. And each of us has different health needs. Yet, the only real proof that interests us is the experience of health itself. Anyone who has been sick knows how good it feels to be well again. The most basic definition of health is the absence of disease. But there is even a higher level of health shown by abundant vitality, mental clarity, good sleep, positive emotions, and endless curiosity and zest for life.

That is the feeling you will enjoy when you achieve real health. My experience with macrobiotics, and the experiences of hundreds of people I have known, have proven that this way of eating and living can give you true health.

Menus

The menus that follow are designed to illustrate typical macrobiotic meals. All the recipes listed can be found in this book and are offered to give you ideas and food choices for better health.

Five-Day Meal Plan

This meal plan is designed for those with existing health concerns where a more limited diet may be helpful. Some macrobiotic counselors recommend this type diet for several months or until improvement is noted, when a broader macrobiotic diet may be enjoyed. Still, if you are suffering from illness, it is suggested that you speak with your health-care advisor.

Breakfasts

Basic Miso Soup, page 20
Boiled Brown Rice, page 27
Bancha Twig Tea, page 217

———◇———

Butternut Squash Miso Soup, page 22
Soft and Sweet Barley with Spelt, page 32
Bancha Twig Tea, page 217

———◇———

Daikon Wakame Miso Soup, page 21
Instant Rice "Muffin," page 29
Bancha Twig Tea, page 217

———— ◇ ————

Watercress Soup, page 23
Hearty Millet Porridge, page 40
Bancha Twig Tea, page 217

———— ◇ ————

Creamy Butternut Squash Soup, page 22
My Favorite Millet Medley, page 38
Bancha Twig Tea, page 217

———— ◇ ————

Lunches

Rice with Scallions and Nori, page 31
Steamed Greens, page 50
Bancha Twig Tea, page 217

———— ◇ ————

Noodles and Broth, page 24
Quick Boiled Vegetables with *Umeboshi Dressing,* page 52, 167
Bancha Twig Tea, page 217

———— ◇ ————

Soft Millet with Cauliflower, page 40
Green Cabbage with Umeboshi Sauce, page 50
Bancha Twig Tea, page 217

———— ◇ ————

Instant Rice "Muffin," page 29
Sesame Collards over Soba, page 48
Rutabaga Pickles, page 103
Bancha Twig Tea, page 217

———— ◇ ————

Quick Quinoa, page 41
Chinese Stir-Fry, page 64
Bancha Twig Tea, page 217

———— ◇ ————

Dinners

Great Northern Bean Soup, page 16
Pressure-Cooked Brown Rice, page 28
Sesame Broccoli, page 61
Dried Daikon and Kombu, page 67
Simple Pressed Salad, page 103

—— ◇ ——

Carrot and Oat Soup, page 23
Basic Azuki Beans, page 71
Pressure-Cooked Brown Rice and Millet, page 29
Hijiki with Ume Dressing, page 82
Steamed Greens, page 50

—— ◇ ——

Lentil Stew, page 77
Pressure-Cooked Brown Rice and Barley, page 28
Kale with Ume Dressing, page 48
Arame Sauté, page 81
Daikon Ume Pickles, page 104

—— ◇ ——

Watercress Soup, page 23
Pressure-Cooked Brown Rice, page 28
Kidney Beans with Miso, page 74
Green Cabbage with Umeboshi Sauce, page 50
Arame with Carrots and Onions, page 82

—— ◇ ——

Anasazi Beans with Kombu, page 70
One-Pot Millet Stew, page 39
Hijiki with Lotus Root and Onions, page 83
Steamed Greens, page 50
Pressed Salad, page 102

—— ◇ ——

Seasonal Changes

In the summer, we naturally want more cooling foods like salads, raw or quickly cooked foods, less oil and salt. Suggestions for summer cooking include:

1. More boiling and steaming; less baking and sautéeing
2. More green vegetables; less root vegetables
3. More tofu instead of beans
4. Less oil, salt, and flour products
5. More grain salads; some raw vegetables
6. More noodles, barley

In the winter we are attracted to more baked goods, hearty stews, and fried foods. Suggestions for winter cooking are:

1. More grains including short-grain brown rice, oats, sweet brown rice, and buckwheat
2. Stronger seasoning with salt, miso, and soy sauce
3. Hearty soups and stews with root vegetables and tempeh
4. Longer cooking times

Summer Menus

Watercress Soup, page 23
Boiled Brown Rice, page 27
Great Greens, page 49
Tabouli Salad, page 91

———— ◇ ————

Noodles and Broth, page 24
Quinoa Salad, page 92
Green Beans Almondine, page 58
Steamed Greens, page 50

———— ◇ ————

Daikon Wakame Miso Soup, page 21
Bulgur with Shiitake Sauce, page 33
Kale with Ume Dressing, page 48
Quick Skillet Corn, page 60

———◇———

Basic Miso Soup, page 20
Bulgur Shiitake Pilaf, page 34
Mexican Chalupas, page 121
Kale with Ume Dressing, page 48

———◇———

═══════════*Winter Menus*═══════════

Pressure-Cooked Kidney Beans and Spelt, page 42
One-Pot Millet Stew, page 39
Saucy Sauerkraut, page 67
Kinpira, page 54

———◇———

Black-Eyed Peas with Sassafras, page 72
Pressure-Cooked Brown Rice, page 28
Scalloped Cauliflower, page 60
Hijiki Onion Sauté, page 84

———◇———

Yellow Split Pea and Barley Soup, page 19
Oat Pilaf, page 41
Pan-Roasted Vegetables, page 55
Teriyaki Shiitake, page 62

———◇———

Special Occasion Menus

These menus are designed for holidays and special occasions when more festive foods are traditionally served.

Red Lentil Soup, page 20
Herbed Quinoa, page 42
Holiday Acorn Squash, page 66
Quick Skillet Corn, page 60
Sea Palm Sauté, page 86
Tofu "Cheesecake," page 178

——— ◇ ———

Carrot and Oat Soup, page 23
Herbed Quinoa, page 42
Lentil Loaf, page 126
Chinese Stir-Fry, page 64
Carrot Cake with *Tofu "Whipped Cream,"* page 173, 196

——— ◇ ———

Green Split Pea and Barley Soup, page 18
Millet "Meatballs" with *Brown Gravy,* page 118, 154
Fiesta Squash, page 65
Carrot Raisin Salad, page 99
Old-Fashioned Corn Bread, page 107
Cherry Pie, page 175

——— ◇ ———

Red Bean Soup, page 17
Texas-Style Polenta, page 36
Savory Rice Loaf, page 116
Broccoli Mushroom Stir-Fry, page 63
Almond Cookies, page 187

——— ◇ ———

Butternut Squash Miso Soup, page 22
Dilled Couscous with Limas, page 37
Leek Sauté, page 59
Broccoli Quiche, page 132
Blueberry Crisp, page 193

——— ◇ ———

The Cooking Environment

Good cooking is a commitment. Realize how important your work is and exactly what you give with the food you cook—your attention, energy, and love. A cook in a kitchen is an alchemist of the highest order—an artist, a scientist, and a healer all rolled into one. You're making beautiful, delicious art. But your art will be eaten and your ingredients will change the contents of people's blood. Your food can restore health; it can change your life and the lives of those you cook for. Your commitment to your cooking is really your willingness to clear away every distraction and focus entirely on what you are doing.

When I'm cooking a meal, I'm concentrating on each ingredient, every chop of my knife, every turn of the vegetables in my skillet. I'm washing my grain and adjusting the flame beneath my pressure cooker for what I feel will be just the right amount of heat. I'm thinking of how to balance the meal—a tasty grain dish with a luscious sauce, some greens and just the right garnish, maybe a bean, a sea vegetable, a sweet baked squash, and a nice dessert. I'm thinking also about color and a variety of tastes and cooking styles—the grain may be pressure cooked, the greens steamed, the squash baked, the seaweed sautéed and simmered. That's a nice balance of foods, colors, and cooking methods. None of this is labor or a forced effort. I'm participating deeply in what I'm doing. I'm right here, right now, cooking this meal; and I'm really enjoying myself.

To give yourself fully to your work, you need the right equipment. This does not mean that you can't adapt or improvise, but you must have the basics in order to focus and enjoy yourself. As you become more familiar with cooking macrobiotic foods and as your budget allows, consider adding some special items. Some items are more important than others, but this list is representative of what you eventually will need to do the job right.

Kitchen range. I strongly recommend a gas range. Electric stoves give food an inferior flavor, and no serious chef would use one. But that dull taste is just a symptom of the deficient power and energy instilled in the food by the electric burner. At a very obvious level, we can see that a gas flame is more vital and alive than an electric burner. That vitality is communicated to your food, so by eating that food you take it in. Fine cooking means learning to appreciate the subtle, yet powerful nature of food and energy.

Saucepans and pots. Consider quality first—after all, what's the point of cooking the best food if you're going to cook it in inferior pots? All my pots are made of stainless steel, cast iron, or good-quality enamel. Cast-iron pots with enamel interiors are among my favorite kitchen tools, and can be used on top of the stove or for baking in the oven. They can be used to cook almost anything, but they are especially good for cooking grains such as quinoa, millet, bulgur, and teff. I can't imagine cooking corn polenta in any other kind of pot. With the lid on, they hold heat and go on cooking the food for another few minutes after the flame is turned off, thereby saving fuel. The pots come in a variety of sizes and colors, making them very attractive and helping to beautify your kitchen. Avoid aluminum or teflon-coated pans. Aluminum is a highly toxic metal that studies show may be linked to Alzheimer's disease and other illnesses. Teflon and cheap metal pots flake or chip into the food. The immune system may react to these chemicals and metals and cause a variety of disorders.

It is important to have pots and pans that you're comfortable with. You will need a variety of sizes, ranging from one quart to eight quarts. The size and number of pots you purchase will depend on how many people you cook for. You'll need a couple of heavy pots for cooking grains and beans and some lighter-weight pots for quick-boiling vegetables. The smaller pots will be used to reheat leftovers and cook smaller portions. The big pots can be used for beans, soups, and noodles, all of which you'll want to cook plenty of and reheat later in the week. Just be sure each pot fits the job you have for it.

Pressure cooker. A pressure cooker locks in the nutrients and the flavor of grain, making it nuttier and fuller-bodied than boiled grain. Beans can be pressure cooked to cut down on the cooking time. A three- or four-quart pressure cooker is ideal for both single people and small families, though you can purchase a variety of sizes. The best pressure cookers are made from stainless steel or enameled steel.

Stainless-steel skillet. In addition to sautéing a variety of foods, a good skillet can be used to stir-fry and steam vegetables. Also, a nine- or ten-inch skillet offers enough room to reheat a grain, a vegetable, and steam some tofu, all at the same time, for a single person who doesn't want to deal with a lot of pots.

Cast-iron skillet. Cast-iron pots leach iron into the food, enriching your food with this essential mineral. They are great for baking corn bread.

Steamer. A steamer is essential for reheating leftover grain and steaming vegetables.

Vegetable knife. I use a knife made of chrome-molybdenum steel that will retain its edge and quality for years. Carbon-steel and stainless-steel knives are also very good. I recommend a rectangular, light, and perfectly balanced knife to provide the most efficient cutting experience you can have. When I first started cooking, I used a regular kitchen cleaver to cut my vegetables. I couldn't figure out why I was so tired from wielding that thing even after a short time. Then I bought a good vegetable knife and realized what a different experience these knives provide; they glide through your vegetables. I use a sharpening rod to keep my knives sharp. You will need one, too.

Wooden spoons. Used for handling food in all kinds of ways, wooden spoons are great because they can't scratch your pans and they're very gentle to vegetables. Having a few of them in a variety of sizes is a good idea.

Tea strainer. I recommend bancha twig tea as a regular beverage and this requires a tea strainer. I use a bamboo strainer for small quantities and a large stainless steel strainer for large quantities.

Vegetable grater. You need both a stainless-steel and a porcelain grater because each has its own use. The steel grater shaves or shreds; the porcelain grater pulverizes, producing more juice than the steel variety. When you're making ginger juice, you want the most juice from the ginger root, so the porcelain grater is the better choice. But when you simply want vegetable shavings, the stainless steel variety is your best bet.

Vegetable brush. Important minerals and vitamins are located at the surface of the vegetable. You don't want to lose those nutrients by peeling them off. Rather, you simply want to clean the vegetable, without bruising the skin. A vegetable brush does that perfectly.

Wooden cutting board. A twelve- by fourteen-inch cutting board is what you need for cutting vegetables.

Heat diffuser. Use a heat diffuser under your pressure cooker or saucepans to spread the heat evenly. It keeps the heat from being concentrated on a specific area, which prevents the foods from burning.

Sushi mats. These are used to make rice rolls and sushi, and to cover your pots while the food inside is allowed to cool. They are essentially bamboo sticks, woven together to form a mat.

Suribachi. This ceramic bowl with a ridged, unglazed inner surface is used with a wooden pestle for grinding seeds and nuts, mashing tofu, puréing miso, and making gomashio and other condiments.

Blender or food processor. This is not a necessity, but very handy — and fast. All kinds of creamy sauces, vegetable fillings, and desserts can be made with a good food processor or blender. I've included a number of recipes that require a food processor.

Glass jars. Tall jars are excellent for storing grains, beans, kuzu, seaweed, nuts, and dried fruit. Food is colorful; it brightens the kitchen and inspires you to use it in all kinds of new and exciting ways.

Measuring cups, spatulas, and ladles. A variety of these are necessary. However, there are a lot of small kitchen gadgets that you can purchase that won't make a difference in your cooking. Avoid filling your kitchen with stuff you don't need. Don't crowd it with a lot of utensils that only get in your way and create chaos.

Rolling pin or pestle from suribachi. You'll need this to roll out pie crusts.

Tea kettle. Use an enamel, glass, or ceramic tea kettle for making tea.

Small salad press. A one- or two-quart salad press is all you need to make salads and pickles. Bigger is not better in this case.

Colander. For washing grains, vegetables, and fruit, a colander is a must.

Large mixing bowl. At least one large mixing bowl is needed for combining ingredients and making salads.

Cookie sheet, cake pans, and pie pans. Again, good-quality tools will last longer, give better flavor to the food, and are better for your health.

It's important to develop a relationship with your equipment. When you use a pot consistently, you get to know it. You know what foods to prepare in that pot, and which ones shouldn't be cooked in it. You rely on the pots and utensils for specific jobs. They develop a certain character and personality. Each of them has its own little history. One day while I was standing in my restaurant kitchen, washing a bunch of pots and utensils, one of my regular customers came back and looked at me amongst all my stainless-steel and iron friends. My customer said, "Margaret, I'll bet there is something unique about each of those pots." I just smiled and said, "You are right—each one is special."

Glossary

Amasake — Sweet drink made from sweet rice and koji, fermented. It may be purchased from natural-food stores.

Arame — Long, thin, black sea vegetable with a mild taste. Customarily prepared as a side dish and served in small quantities, about one tablespoon per person. Arame may be purchased from natural-food stores and mail-order suppliers.

Baking powder — A leavening agent that causes baked foods to rise by the action of acid and alkaline. Most brands of baking powder contain aluminum compounds; look for an aluminum-free brand. Aluminum-free baking powder may be purchased from natural-food stores and some supermarkets.

Bancha twig tea — Beverage made from the twigs of tea bushes. Bancha tea twigs may be purchased from natural-food stores and mail-order suppliers.

To make bancha twig tea, bring two quarts water to a boil. Add two tablespoons twigs and simmer five minutes. Turn flame off and let steep about five minutes before serving. Twigs may be reused. Add a little more water and a few fresh twigs.

Barley malt syrup — Natural sweetener made from whole barley or barley and corn. It may be purchased from natural-food stores.

Bulgur — Wheat that has been partially cooked, then dried and cracked. Bulgur may be purchased from natural-food stores and some supermarkets.

Chapati — Flat wheat bread, common in India. Chapatis may be purchased from natural-food stores and Indian grocery stores.

Daikon radish — Long white radish. Daikon radish may be purchased from natural-food stores and some supermarkets.

Dulse — A reddish-purple sea vegetable, rich in iron and other minerals. Dulse can be eaten raw in salads, steamed, fried, or used in soups. It may be purchased from natural-food stores and mail-order suppliers.

Fu — Dried wheat gluten. Fu may be purchased from natural-food stores and mail-order suppliers.

Ginger juice — The juice of fresh ginger root. Fresh ginger root is grated on the finest teeth of a grater. The resulting pulp is squeezed to extract the juice. Fresh ginger root may be purchased in supermarkets. *See also* Vegetable grater, page 214.

Gomashio — A condiment composed of sesame seeds and salt, roasted and crushed together and served sprinkled over grains and vegetables, about one teaspoonful per serving. Gomashio can be made in varying proportions, from ten parts sesame seeds for each part salt, to eighteen parts sesame seeds to one part salt. It may be purchased from natural-food stores and mail-order suppliers but it is better made at home.

To make gomashio, wash one cup unhulled sesame seeds; rinse in strainer and drain. Heat a skillet; add sesame seeds and one teaspoon sea salt. Roast seeds and salt over low flame until seeds turn darker in color and give off a nutty aroma. Place roasted seeds and salt in a suribachi and grind the seeds with the pestle slowly but firmly until the seeds are about half crushed. Allow to cool completely and place in a covered jar to store. *See also* Suribachi, page 215.

Granulated garlic — Dried and coarsely ground garlic that dissolves quickly without lumping when added to food. Garlic powder has a tendency to lump. Granulated garlic may be purchased from natural-food stores and some supermarkets.

Granulated onion — Dried and coarsely ground onion that dissolves quickly without lumping when added to food. Granulated onion may be purchased from natural-food stores and some supermarkets.

Hijiki (Hiziki) — A black sea vegetable shaped in long strands, rich in a wide variety of minerals, especially calcium. It may be purchased from natural-food stores and mail-order suppliers.

Kanten — Seaweed gelatin, used in making kanten gelatin desserts or aspics. Kanten is also called agar agar. It may be purchased from natural-food stores and mail-order suppliers.

Kinpira — A cooking style. Vegetables, especially burdock and carrots, are finely cut at an angle and sautéed with soy sauce.

Koji — A grain inoculated with spores of *aspergillus oryzae* to create a culture which is then used to make miso, soy sauce, amasake, and other fermented foods. Koji may be purchased from natural-food stores and mail-order suppliers.

Kombu — Highly nutritious sea vegetable used in stews, soups, and in cooking beans. Kombu may be purchased from natural-food stores and mail-order suppliers.

Kuzu — Powdered starch made from the root of the hardy kudzu plant, used as a thickening agent and as a medicinal food. It may be purchased from natural-food stores and mail-order suppliers.

Mirin — Sweet rice cooking wine. Naturally fermented mirin is made of sweet rice, koji, and water. Naturally fermented mirin may be purchased from natural-food stores and mail-order suppliers.

Miso — Fermented and aged soybean paste, made from soybeans, salt, koji, and barley or rice; or some other bean and grain. Rich in digestive enzymes and friendly bacteria. Miso is used as a base for soups, stews, sauces, and gravies. It may be purchased from natural-food stores and mail-order suppliers.

Mochi — Sweet rice steamed and pounded. Mochi may be purchased from natural-food stores and mail-order suppliers.

Mugi — Barley.

Natto — Fermented soybean condiment, served with rice or other grains, or in soup. Natto may be purchased from Oriental grocery stores and some natural-food stores.

Nishime — A cooking style. Vegetables are cut in large pieces at an extreme angle, cooked slowly, and seasoned with soy sauce.

Nori — Thin sheets of seaweed, highly nutritious, often used to make sushi and rice balls. Nori may be purchased from natural-food stores and mail-order suppliers.

Polenta — Cornmeal. Polenta may be purchased from natural-food stores, mail-order suppliers, and some supermarkets.

Raspberry vinegar — Vinegar flavored with raspberries and used in marinades. It may be purchased from natural-food stores and supermarkets.

Rice balls — Rice shaped into compact balls and covered with toasted nori or gomashio. In the center, a small piece of umeboshi plum is added for flavor.

Rice syrup — A sweetener made from malted brown rice. Rice syrup may be purchased from natural-food stores and mail-order suppliers.

Sassafras — Dried and powdered sassafras leaves are known as filé and may be found in the spice section of the supermarket.

Sauerkraut — Natural sauerkraut is made from shredded cabbage fermented with salt. It can be made at home or purchased from natural-food stores.

Seitan — Wheat gluten cooked with soy sauce. Seitan is rich in protein and is sometimes called *wheat meat* because it has a similar consistency to meat. Seitan may be made at home or purchased from natural-food stores.

Sesame butter — Ground, roasted, unhulled sesame seeds

made into a paste or butter and used in spreads, sauces, and dressings. Sesame butter may be purchased from natural-food stores.

Shio kombu — Condiment made of kombu, soaked, cut into squares, and cooked with soy sauce.

Soba — Noodles made from buckwheat flour or a combination of buckwheat flour and whole-wheat flour. Soba may be purchased from natural-food stores and mail-order suppliers.

Soy sauce — Natural soy sauce is made from whole soybeans, wheat, koji, and sea salt and is aged naturally, without chemicals, for one to two years. Natural soy sauce may be purchased from natural-food stores and mail-order suppliers.

Spelt — An ancient grain that looks and tastes like wheat. It can be substituted for wheat in most recipes and can be milled into flour for baking. Spelt may be purchased from natural-food stores and mail-order suppliers.

Sushi — Rice and vegetables wrapped in toasted nori and sliced in rounds.

Sushi nori — Sheets of nori that have been toasted. Sushi nori may be purchased from natural-food stores and mail-order suppliers.

Tahini — Paste made from ground, hulled sesame seeds. The sesame seeds may be toasted or raw. Tahini may be purchased from natural-food stores.

Tamari — Liquid by-product of miso production that is generally not available. The term *tamari* is sometimes mistakenly used to refer to natural soy sauce and wheat-free soy sauce.

Tekka — A dry, powdered condiment made from burdock, carrot, lotus root, and miso. It is often served sprinkled over grain. Tekka may be purchased from natural-food stores and mail-order suppliers.

Tempura — Style of cooking using batter and deep-frying.

Toasted sesame oil — Oil extracted from toasted sesame seeds. Toasted sesame oil may be purchased from natural-food stores and mail-order suppliers.

Tofu — Smooth, white cakes of pressed curd made from soybeans and a coagulant, preferably nigari. Tofu is rich in protein and calcium. Tofu made with nigari may be purchased from natural-food stores.

Udon — Noodles made from sifted wheat. Udon may be purchased from natural-food stores and mail-order suppliers.

Ume sho kuzu — A drink traditionally used to promote and strengthen good digestion and to restore energy.

To make ume sho kuzu, place one cup water in a saucepan and bring to a simmer. Dissolve one heaping teaspoon kuzu in one tablespoon cold water. Whisk the dissolved kuzu into the simmering water. Reduce flame as low as possible. Stir constantly to avoid lumping until the liquid becomes transparent, about one minute. Stir in one-half an umeboshi plum (chopped), one-half teaspoon natural soy sauce, and one-quarter teaspoon ginger juice (squeezed from grated fresh ginger root).

Umeboshi — A variety of Japanese plum pickled in salt and beefsteak (shiso) leaves. Umeboshi is used as a condiment and as a medicinal food. It may be purchased from natural-food stores and mail-order suppliers.

Wakame — Leafy seaweed, highly nutritious, used in soup and stews. Wakame may be purchased from natural-food stores and mail-order suppliers.

Index

Cookbooks and Videos
from the George Ohsawa Macrobiotic Foundation

As Easy as 1, 2, 3 - Pamela Henkel and Lee Koch; 1990; 176 pp; $6.95. Quick, easy, and delicious recipes from the founders of the Macro Dome Cooking School in Wisconsin.

Basic Macrobiotic Cooking - Julia Ferré; 1987; 288 pp; $9.95. Complete guide to the procedures of cooking whole grains and fresh vegetables using familiar foods, easily obtained. Over 300 recipe examples.

The Calendar Cookbook - Cornellia Aihara; 1979; 232 pp; $14.95. Features over 370 recipes and a balanced menu for every day of the year.

Cooking with Rachel - Rachel Albert; 1989; 328 pp; $12.95. Creative gourmet vegetarian macrobiotic recipes to entertain guests, dazzle friends and relatives, and excite the most discerning palates.

The Do of Cooking - Cornellia Aihara; 1982; 232 pp: $19.95. This great source of inspiration contains more than 460 seasonal recipes, a wild-vegetable section, kitchen hints, and much more.

The First Macrobiotic Cookbook - *Revised Edition*; 1985; 140 pp; $9.95. Originally published as *Zen Cookery* in 1964. The revised edition is the second printing under the new title with spiral binding and new easy-to-use format.

How to Prepare a Macrobiotic Meal - Cornellia Aihara; 1990; video; 60 minutes; $35.00. Displays the spirit and experience of Cornellia Aihara as she creates a macrobiotic meal step-by-step. Filmed at the Vega Study Center. Recipe booklet enclosed.

The Naturally Healthy Gourmet - Margaret Lawson with Tom Monte; 1994; 232 pp; $14.95. Everyday food becomes company fare with Margaret's secrets of practical, wholesome, gourmet cooking. This book is sure to spark your creative zeal for natural-foods cooking.

To order or to obtain a complete macrobiotic book catalog, contact:

George Ohsawa Macrobiotic Foundation
1511 Robinson Street, Oroville, CA 95965
(916) 533-7702; fax (916) 533-7908